Align

attract,
accept, and
accelerate
abundance

A COMPILATION BY MISTILEI WRISTON

Align
Attract, accept, and accelerate abundance
Compiled by Misti Wriston
CampGroundTBD Publishing

Published by CampGroundTBD Publishing, Mena, Arkansas

Editor: Cheryl Roberts Oliver

Cover and Interior design:
Davis Creative Publishing Partners,
CreativePublishingPartners.com

Names: Wriston, Misti, compiler.
Title: Align : attract, accept, and accelerate abundance / a compilation by Misti
        Wriston.
Description: Mena, Arkansas : CampGroundTBD Publishing, [2022]
Identifiers: ISBN: 979-8-9863594-3-4 (paperback) | 979-8-9863594-4-1 (ebook) | 979-
        8-9863594-5-8 (hardback) | LCCN: 2022918381
Subjects: LCSH: Peace of mind--Literary collections. | Peace of mind--Anecdotes. |
        Self-consciousness (Awareness)--Literary collections. | Self-consciousness
        (Awareness)--Anecdotes. | Stress management--Literary collections. | Stress
        management--Anecdotes. | Control (Psychology)-- Literary collections.
        | Control (Psychology)--Anecdotes. | Self-esteem--Literary collections. |
        Self-esteem--Anecdotes. | LCGFT: Self-help publications. | BISAC: SELF-HELP
        / Motivational & Inspirational. | SELF-HELP / Personal Growth / Happiness. |
        SELF-HELP / Substance Abuse & Addictions / Alcohol.
Classification: LCC: BF637.P3 W75 2022 | DDC: 158.1/02--dc23

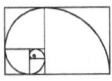

Dedication

*This book is dedicated to the young man that will
make me a grandmother early December 2022.*

*It is also dedicated to my deceased father.
I am grateful for the relationship I will
now be able to have with both!*

This book is dedicated to you.

This book is dedicated to me.

This book is dedicated to God.

Mistilei

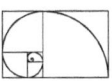

Table of Contents

"Everything
in life is tbd:
to be determined,
to be designed."

— Mistilei

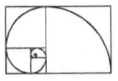

Mistilei Wriston

Introduction

I am what you might call a *Hard-Core Lover of Alignment*. It has been the best thing I have ever learned about living my life and making choices. The way alignment is defined varies from person-to-person and across all walks of life. The way people identify when they are mis-aligned or out of alignment varies just as much. Alignment is very personal. It comes down to your relationship to a certain course of action based on where you are at this second, and then the next second. For me, it is the balance of my three parts: body, mind, and soul and whether or not those three parts agree, based on my current trajectory? It sounds so simple.

And yet we all (and I do mean all) find ourselves out of alignment at times in various aspects of life. The reason hindsight is 20/20 is we can see how we could have aligned ourselves in various situations, but only after we've experienced them. Hindsight alone doesn't change anything. The better alternative is to learn to actively monitor our alignment, continuously and honestly.

It is my experience that the faster I identify when I've veering from my alignment, the more magic I experience when I correct my path. I know I cannot avoid misalignment, so the goal is to correct my course as soon as I notice it and to identify where I got off course. I admit I have had many areas of my life where I knew I needed to make changes but was not ready to see the path. I was not ready to be in alignment. I was stuck in the no-way-out mindset. Now I understand that being resistant to ANY possible outcome was why I was stuck or frustrated or unable to see clearly. My vision was clouded by my misalignment and desire to stay in a space I believed I knew. I was so out of alignment; it had blinded me to the facts.

Alignment went from motivational posters to my life's dedication. Exposure to each new level reveals the magic is exponentially better and more intoxicating than the level before. I have learned to apply the test of alignment to every area of my life. When I listen to the answers, I see infinite improvement. When I feel myself begin to slip or my life becomes chaotic, I recognize I have veered. Then, upon my realignment, the magic blossoms once again. As I mastered the skill of correction, I noticed I was attracting new people, new friends and new clients who attributed alignment to their current success in any and all areas. I noticed that in this new circle, the magic of like-minded people in proximity is an intoxicating wonder to witness! It is an example of alignment with others.

It is my request that you will read this book cover to cover at your leisure and let each author's words swim around in your mind, excite your senses and open to new ways to align with your best life, your true self! I know what alignment has done for me. I know what it has done for those around me, and I know what it can do for you. Please enjoy a brief look at what alignment means to these incredible authors.

With love,
Mistilei

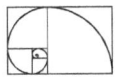

Jillian Wallace

Intuition

Trust Your Gut

"To trust your gut means to have confidence in yourself that you know what's best. It's trusting that your unsettled feelings mean something and are worth considering. There's a reason that you feel bothered about a situation or layer of your life—an intensity that will only grow the more it is swept under the rug."[1]

What does intuition mean to you? How do you define it? Imagine if you could decide that you were going to *stop* believing you *don't* know what you know. Put positively, imagine if you believed *you know what you know*, if you were confident that what you felt in your gut was actually wisdom acquired from experiences imbued with universal energy and lifetimes of memory.

Seriously, think about that! Try that reality on and see how it fits. What if you just knew you knew and you trusted your gut about anything and everything, from the restaurant that you want to eat at, to hiring someone at your company, to who to have as partners and friends, and to making big financial decisions? Sounds simple! I'm sure some of you are thinking that you already do that, but do you? I mean do you really?[2]

The reasoning behind the phrase *trust your gut* isn't random. It's the result of the incredible gut-brain connection we humans have. Our physical bodies are quite literally wired to experience the world through our nervous systems. One of these systems is our enteric nervous system, which has a rich network of over one hundred million nerve cells in the gut. This makes it almost impossible for us to ignore, and yet every day that's what we do. We decide we don't know. We talk ourselves out of listening to the nagging gut feeling. At best, we tell ourselves our bodies are wrong; at worst, we don't even notice what our bodies are saying. We intentionally decide not to trust ourselves, and then we go about seeking answers outside ourselves. We seek gurus, self-help books, advice from friends, comfort, and escape. We do about anything to *not listen to our own body expressing and experiencing*. Here's a thought: What if that's the better part of us, the smarter part of us? So why don't we listen?

I think it's trust. When we as human beings lack trust in ourselves, we make poor decisions and lose touch with our physical bodies. Or we bifurcate our feelings and thoughts and remain paralyzed with ambivalence. When this is our reality, we tend to not take action, and we miss out on opportunities and close our hearts to the greatest gift of life: love. This shows up in many ways, but the worst way is lack of love for ourselves.

Let's go on a journey together. First, draw on a deep childlike faith, then imagine that anything is possible. Imagine for a second that you really could trust that you do know what you want, what you need, and what is real for you. Now think about that knowing. Where is it? How big is it? How big are you? Does your nervous system that is both within and beyond your physical flesh and bones touch the borders of your knowing, then melt into and become a greater *wisdom*? Are you more of yourself when you are in touch with your body? The answer is yes. Embodiment is at the core of intuition. When you accept and accelerate all of your intuition, you feel more in touch with the universe, and therein with all of creation.

Try this exercise: Tell yourself you don't know. You can't be trusted. You have no confidence. How large or small are you feeling when you don't know? When you feel disconnected? When you feel isolated, powerless, or you're suffering? If you don't know what's real with your body, you don't know what's real with your life. The opposite is also true: knowing what is physically real about your body can help you accept reality. The challenge is not letting the mind take over. Overthinking causes countless restrictions.

Intuition is being all of you. Deciding to trust in yourself, knowing you know what's best for yourself, creates sovereignty, and sovereignty creates magic. You decide to have sovereignty; therefore, you determine how much access you have to the abundance of energy and sheer magic of creation. Just decide that you know, then act as if you can't screw it up.

Everybody knows somebody who has (or they have themselves) experienced utter betrayal. Betrayal can be traumatizing. It can make us lose faith in ourselves and shake our reality, but how many times have you heard (after the fact) someone acknowledging, "I knew it. I knew that SOB was a cheater! I saw the lipstick on the shirt. I saw the credit card bill."

Sometimes we choose to explain it away. We buy a bullshit story from our partner about where they were, or about a grade on a test from our children, or how far along a coworker is on a mutual project. We buy it but because we want to buy it. We don't want to know the truth. Herein lies the experience of ignorance being bliss. We want to ignore our intuition and shut off our energetic and physical being, closing down for our own comfort because being at one with ourselves feels too painful, or we have been told we are too much, too big, and we seek to make ourselves smaller for acceptance. Ouch.

What if it was really as easy as deciding? Rumi would say, "What you seek is seeking you." Winifred Gallagher, author of *Rapt: Attention and the Focused Life*,[3] advanced her theory that you are what you pay attention to,[4] that you in fact create what you pay attention to. What are you paying attention to in your daily life? What are you attracting with your focus?

I urge you: decide today to be *all of you*. Take up space and live your authentic truth. Experience your truth in your body as you read these words. Experience all one hundred million nerve cells in your gut telling you that you can trust with absolute certainty that you know what's up about every area in your life. You know who's really got to go, what conversations need to be had, what decisions you need to make. You also know where you're falling short. Where you need to take more accountability and respond and act accordingly. Your gut feelings reflect a physical experience of holistic truth.

How much magic are you OK with? Do you want just a little bit of magic, or do you want the kind of mystical life that submits to the wildest desires of the universe in unapologetic alignment, courageous truth, and reverent love? Make a decision and cut off any other option. That is when you realize the universe will conspire to help you.

We experience the most incredibly perfect timing of manifestation. Things seem to become effortless and just fall into our laps. Just like that, we're in alignment with what is true for ourselves as we become one with the wave of life's flow.

Today, give up the good and go for the great. You might meet the love of your life, find a new career, or end up in some totally unique situation that created the perfect opportunity for growth or financial abundance. Or—and here's the real part—it will never happen as long as you keep talking yourself out of it. Fighting the current of life only wears you out.

One of the greatest lessons I needed to learn in life was how to gracefully let go of something not meant for me. This lesson has showed up many times until it set me free as the truth tends to. Many people misinterpret integrity. They think it is being of character. Integrity is truly being all of you for better or worse. Believe in yourself, your intuition, and discover a life full of sexy, rich, volcanic fortune, abundant passion, and utter fulfillment. Breathe into the here and now, if for only now, and follow your intuition.

Jillian Joy Wallace is a sales leader and world traveler. She is passionate about energy—from owning a residential solar energy business to practicing energy systems in and around our physical bodies—and how it shapes our reality. As an author, she hopes to be a beacon to electrify, energize, and inspire others to live with intentional magic. She is a feminine force and a creative coach. If you enjoyed this chapter, you may find the full story of intuition and relationships of interest. Check out "The Blue Couch Conversation" at *www.thebluecouchconversation.com*. Whether you are single and ready to mingle or in a committed relationship, "The Blue Couch Conversations" will help you create the blueprint to start a new relationship or revive an existing one with intention. So, here's to lovers: may we know them, and may we be them.

www.thebluecouchconversation.com

1 Courtney Ciandella, "What It Means to Trust Your Gut," The Wallflower Blog (blog), December 21, 2021, https://studio-wallflower.com/what-it-means-to-trust-your-gut/.

2 Yes, You Should Trust Your Gut (Here's How) - One Love Foundation (joinonelove.org)

3 https://www.amazon.com/Rapt-Attention-Focused-Winifred-Gallagher-ebook/dp/B001V6P12E/ref=tmm_kin_swatch_0?_encoding=UTF8&qid=1536651050&sr=8-1

4 Francisco Sáez, "You Are What You Pay Attention To," FacileThings (blog). Retrieved from https://facilethings.com/blog/en/you-are-what-you-pay-attention-to/.

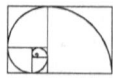

Mistilei Wriston

Me myself and I

Aligning with My Soul Purpose

Q, short for Conquistador, the supreme rooster in charge, is crowing out-side my window. He knows exactly where I sleep. The sun will not be up for hours. He does not care how that rumor got started. I will need a robe this morning as the weather is just barely starting to chill. My feet are both excited and hesitant as the cold, wet grass passes my ankle on the way to the barn. Maybe I will trim the grass today. Maybe not.

I let the small chickens out first. These tiny three need a head start and always need a few moments of Momma time. I snuggle them before starting our day. Jenny the Guinea is nosing around, sounding like she needs WD40. After chicken cuddle time, I let the rest of the lady flock out, all named Chickita. Single file, they waddle down their plank and the parade begins. They will race me, although I am in no hurry, to the front of the property where the food bucket now resides. I have given up on keeping the racoons out of the chicken barn and just keep the food in the garage. We all seem to enjoy the long walk in the morning across the property. I eventually meet them there, wade through them and begin putting out handfuls of feed. I love this time and the sounds they make. It reminds me of my children nursing when they were infants and even how Hayden sounds now when he gets the perfect bottle.

As I move the bales and fill the water, clean the roost, and do the chores, I am impressed by my strength. Less than two years ago, I cried because I had to carry a five-gallon water bottle by myself after being dumped and almost killed by someone I should have never gone on a second date with. I am *actually* strong now. I never imagined, at fifty-five, I'd be a person who would admire her body in the reflection and have words like strength come to mind.

The morning is part of my spiritual practice; the timing and the weather are not always optimal. The day starts when it starts no matter what, and my body responds. People say they could not bear the heat, cold, weather, timing, whatever is required to do what I do. I simply do not acknowledge the heat or cold. It is not relevant to my to-do list. The weather is simply the weather. I don't focus on these things.

The animals and I know one another, trust one another. I know when something is off and they do too. If I try to pretend I am fine while tending to them, they will act like they have never seen me before and frustration and chaos will follow. When I am present with them, it is as if they hear and respond to my thoughts. We play together. They follow me. I do my work. The bales are heavy and yet I lift them. I could drag them but I am stronger than that and I want to be even stronger. I carry heavy shit every day. And then I leave other heavy stuff that doesn't matter to be done by others or whenever I feel like it. I keep my strength up and have nothing to prove. I stop and watch them play when I feel like it.

Once the flock is preoccupied with their morning snacks, I head to the pond, alone. The smoke will be coming off the water for the next ninety minutes. I am almost incapable of looking away. I have given up trying. The pond is a crystal ball for me. I find it that magical. I set an intention. I stare into her and the answers appear with absolute clarity. Sometimes, I simply sit and cry to her, for no reason it seems other than we both need it and I don't question me anymore.

I hear my son waking up inside, ready for his bottle. He is twenty-seven and mentally and developmentally around six months old. He and I communicate only through our energy. Our last year and half together exclusively has increased my ability to "understand" him exponentially. I think tuning in with him and learning to hear him increased my ability to hear the animals as well. I freely admit the animals and birds speak to me. I moved off of a mountain thanks to a copperhead and a dragonfly. I don't question me anymore. I began speaking to my dead dad and very dead grandmothers thanks to a lady I saw wiggling her fingers around in a Facebook video talking about energy. I don't question me anymore.

Every day that I spend time in this beautiful space, staring into the morning mist as the sun starts to peak, I receive gifts. I am able to flip mental channels and see possible outcomes for my life and the tiniest changes it would take to change an entire lifetime. Once I stop to look at one option a little longer, the pond brings such clarity to the vision. I can see it, taste it, hear it, feel the moment happening. The less I question myself, the clearer things became. It seems impossible as the unknown was the very thing I feared, and as it turns out, diving into the unknown was the key to being released from my imagined prisons!

The more magic that occurs in my life, the easier it is to feel when I am at one of those intersections, where I can make one single choice and change everything. Now that I can identify *those type of moments*, those moments of alignment, I can easily act on them rather than missing out in indecision. I now see how easy decision making is when I am in alignment. The pond helps and I don't question that.

Shortly after moving to my oasis, standing in this very spot, I received the ability to feel when I had already made the changes. This current moment IS THE RESULT of that. I began to have flashbacks of my life when I made decisions that seems impossible at the time, yet somehow I had the ability to decide and do! I had never known why I had strength in those moments. The connections were starting to form and questions were arising. I could see the magic unfolding while my brain tried to catch up and make sense. I am being shown why I chose my parents. I am shown where I protected myself from my own future.

I hold certain beliefs. I believe we choose our parents. I believe my children chose me. I believe Hayden specifically chose me as he knew I was just the Warrior Princess needed to stop the generational trauma, and he was the only one that could keep my flying-kite personality from getting caught in a tree. He keeps me tethered to the ground, so I could serve in my true calling when the time came. The time is now, my grandchild is on the way. I can see him when I gaze across the pond, playing on a beach that does not exist on the property yet. I have more respect for Hayden now for his choice to be here, now, for picking this family, than I ever imagined.

I also know my family has a long history of familial sexual abuse and secrets and my children have it on both sides as well. The pond showed me that although I had done all the work on the abuse and other inappropriate parenting in my childhood, I still did not understand why I would choose to be born into a family with sexual abuse. There was still a part of the inner child that felt shame in picking that type of family, as if I had entrapped someone or held some blame. I had not been aware of that misplaced shame until now. I was shown a very clear image while meditating on the edge of this pond and a lifetime of shame I was not even aware of, was released with the mist.

My daughter is pregnant with my first grandchild. With no hesitancy, I can tell you if Jesus Christ himself came to me and said, In order to save that Baby Bee from being molested, there is only one way. It requires you go back and be that small child again and go through the life you just led and I will bring you back here, to the place of perfection you call your life, fifty-five years from today. I am gone! DONE! No hesitation. This will end! I have committed to this. There is no other reason I would go back. I love my life, but for this, I would go without hesitation! I have absolute clarity.

The pond played a beautiful, tragic movie for me to enjoy. Not only would I go back, but it's clear, I already have. *We* already have. We agreed to this. Hayden kept me on the right track to complete the task. My daughter is making the miracle baby we were told she could not make because we did the work. The clarity is serenely calming. There is no longer shame or guilt hidden, as all of me sees that we have done the most beautiful thing and we live in paradise today because I listened to me, as did the other balls of light I call my family. We have been brave. We have stopped the trauma and released the toxic waste left behind because we were never victims. We made a decision to end the darkness and BECOME THE LIGHT for this entire bloodline. This is what it took: a moment of clarity that occurred as I felt layers of generational guilt breaking away, brick by brick. The earlier version of myself that I have been sent back to chaperone while I stare at a pond now, was only the first of the line to be freed from this. All those before are also freed by this clarity. Shame is replaced with family pride. We did the work.

I listen to me now, even the quietest whisper, especially as I stand here and watch the mist leave the surface of the water and return to the air. I spend less time wondering why my lessons were so hard, why they required that I scream at myself or even worse, waited for someone else to scream that I was out of alignment and unable to hear the me in me. I simply stay in a space where I can hear now.

I walk back to the house, observing the water marks in the grass where my feet walked an hour before. The sun is up and warming my skin and the dew shimmers like crystals on the grass. The dogs are barking and ready for their puppy pile. I begin my day in a place of gratitude and alignment. I live in magic.

I do not question me anymore. My dear friend Buttercup says "I don't keep GOD waiting. I'm head over heels in love with GOD…which is you, which is me and which is everywhere." I will add, I do not keep Me waiting, ever; it is my agreement with the God in me! All that is needed is to be conscious of my personal alignment. Me, myself and I, along with God, knowing what to do.

Career entrepreneur Mistilei Wriston sold her highly-ranked insurance and financial services franchise after three decades to live in nature, care for her disabled son, grow organic food, raise animals, and simplify her life. Her professional awakening created *campgroundtbd publishing*, aligning her passion and purpose. A two-time, #1 Amazon International Best Selling author, Mistilei believes everyone has a unique story and a calling to share and connect. She recognized that honest, transparent stories change lives. Mistilei coaches those who struggle with misalignment, writer's block, addictions, body image and behavior paralysis by removing perceived limiting beliefs and allowing a space to explore alignment. She encourages those who are ready to share their voice, write their chapter, then see it published along with other courageous and visionary individuals. The chapter is the gift to the world. The growth of each author is a gift to Mistilei. She assists with alignment virtually and with in-person retreats at her beautiful property in Western Arkansas.

calendly.com/campgroundtbd/30min
www.facebook.com/MistileiWriston/

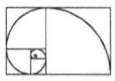

Julia Caton

The Power In a Name

I am now Julia Irene Caton, previously known by the married last name of Parks. It has taken me fifty-one years to arrive at a place where I can go back and really begin the process of healing the injured child who once held this name. Through years of inner and therapeutic work, acceptance, and acknowledgements, I have chosen to go deeper still. Now I return as an adult to let my inner child know she is safe, secure, and stronger than she ever knew. In her fears, she was a fierce fighter. Her bravest attempts to survive shaped me into the woman I am today. This Julia knows who she is and to whom she belongs, and my gratitude for the younger versions of me are deeper than a soul's existence. The name I have chosen to take back will never be silenced, shushed, or allowed to feel or act small. This is what alignment creates in us—a knowing, a testifying of the uniqueness of the self.

Funny story based on the above process, I was second in line to go before the judge as I stood in the courtroom to finalize my return to the name I received at birth. When I walked up with Ms. Sassy, the judge paused and seriously stumbled over her words. Her eyes went from hard to all shiny and giddy. She finally smiled and said, "I am distracted by your dog. She is so pretty." I told her what Ms. Sassy does for me as a medically trained service dog, and about the happiness she brings to the world around us and myself. The bailiffs' faces held pure joy.

The judge asked the remaining questions, and some tears were shed in the courtroom while I told the reasons why my name change was important to me and why I was able to do it at this time in my life. Then, just like that, Parks was changed to Caton. My petition was granted. I don't know if Ms. Sassy and I were the best things that happened in the court room that day, but we definitely spread some excitement and caused some extra smiles.

▽ ▽ ▽ ▽ ▽

Sassafras EverLee Quintessence Parks, "Ms. Sassy," has dedicated her life to service. After training with the best in Oklahoma at Glad Wags, Ms. Sassy has been in the medical field providing care for seizure and allergy detection. Her daily passions and tasks within the fields of medical and mental health are located in Tulsa, Oklahoma. She enjoys winning competitions in grace and poise, as well as traveling. She models and is building her social media presence. The human to her left is Julia Caton, her trusted companion.

Sassy.parks@yahoo.com
www.facebook.com/profile.php?id=100086205427079
www.tiktok.com/@juliaiparks?_t=8WFpQh85C8J&_r=1

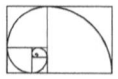

Julia Caton

Authenticity of the Soul

The "I am" Understanding

Have you ever been asked, "Who are you?" The majority of us answer this with a litany of what we do, what we have accomplished or failed at, how we identify with the roles we have assumed, or how others have dictated our lives through lived and unlived expectations. It is as though the very idea of answering this profound question, will trap us into being forever defined by our answer; thus, we continue to avoid the question. We distance and distract ourselves, ultimately remaining trapped by ideas, expressions, and pathways that are anything but authentically who we were divinely designed to be.

When curiosity allows us to play with the "Who are you?" question, the inquiry can be a powerful beacon guiding us to engage and be utterly exposed to the truth that lies within the core of our being. For me, the question demanded that I come face-to-face with my own fears, ideals, beliefs, and expectations. This story is about my journey of stepping bravely into an exploration of the words, "Who are you?" and allowing it to transform into my personal quest for answers to the real question, "Who am I?"

In the process of answering this question, I recognize that each of us is responsible for answering it in our own way and to use whatever modalities enable us to dive deeply into the most frightening thing of all: the unknown. The drive to further understand the depth of myself brought me into contact with a shaman known as Big River John, known to me as friend and soul brother. He is a gifted shaman, called to facilitate plant and other earth medicines that aid those who journey with them into achieving incredible mental, intellectual, and spiritual insights. I'm sure his description of what he does and provides would be far more eloquent than what I am writing here, but this story is about my experience with the question, "Who am I?" I am grateful to have benefited from the extraordinary messages of San Pedro, the Master Teacher and Healer,[5] and Bufo, the God Molecule or Toad Medicine.[5]

The exact process of the Bufo ceremony is sacred, and I have chosen not to include the messages of freedom presented by Mother San Pedro within this chapter, but instead, will begin at the first meditation where I set my intent for Bufo. Having never experienced any plant or earth medicine prior to that evening, I had no expectations except to surrender myself to the medicine, the Teacher, and the raw, most intricate and foundational aspects of myself, all without knowing how or what that would mean.

The pipe was placed at my lips while I sat on the mattress on the floor. I heard the words from John, "Breath in deeply…" I did, and as his words passed somewhere through my conscious brain, I felt my body being reclined, then heard John's words echoing in my ears, "Now surrender." The world I knew before hearing those words was gone as I was taken toward a multitude of tunnels that had no end. It seemed as though, I could reach out and touch each of the presented options, and yet, somehow, I knew I had become them. There was no separation from the various corridors that were in front of me, because each was an intricate part, an essence of myself.

I heard a rumbling, a deep voice akin to what I have since come to recognize as All Knowledge. I became a mixture of expanded space, deep abiding darkness, all that is, will be, or ever was. I was beckoned to ask my questions: "What is fear? Will I always feel it?" I called out, "Am I fear?" Until this moment I had always lived my life in constant states of hyperawareness, knowing my adrenals, nervous system, and mental state were worn down as a result of abuses, both from perpetrators and from myself. It was important for me to find out if this was all I was intended to be—*someone in a state of constant fear.*

Without a beat of time or a whisper of sound, I was instantly rushed to a series of alcoves with gates or door-like barriers preventing me from knowing the contents of the other side. There I stood pondering the exquisite expanse of all that ever was, all the while marveling at the realization that I stood in the realm of great nothingness. There the voice of Bufo instructed, "Choose your path."

The option to choose almost seemed trivial compared to the depth of understanding that flooded my being. There was no wrong choice; each offered a perfect option. Each alcove offered a different direction down a path of different learning, but all would provide what I desired to know as this *being* or version of myself, standing at the gates. There I intentionally chose what was the hardest, most terrifying path of those presented. I instinctively knew if I wanted the answers to my questions, I had to first comprehend that only I could choose what and where I wanted to learn. This was my first lesson: I must choose. My second lesson: whatever my choice, it would be perfect for me during this specific existence.

In a swoosh of time, I found myself in the corridor of creation. I saw myself being formed, birthed, going through the developmental stages of an infant, toddler, and then pausing at the age of nine. I heard my mother's voice, her initial rejection of me; saw the extreme abuses from kin and strangers, the neglect, and the silences; felt the pains, the rush of more rejections, and the development of fears and phobias. I remembered having to shut down aspects of myself. I wanted to hide from the mortal experiences I endured. I was both nine years old and ageless, standing in the vastness before the experience of Bufo, screaming, "Is this fear? Will I always be afraid? Who am I if I am not afraid?"

As though embraced by invisible arms of comfort and peace, I heard the responsive words flow through me: "...and what if it is? Would you have chosen differently?" Looking even deeper down the path I had chosen, I responded with my voice of truth and an eternal knowing smile. "No."

Who am I? Who are you? As I ponder these very questions with the knowledge I gained from the profound experience of Bufo, I state this:

We are everything and nothing at all; we are all time and yet no time; we are the source of all knowledge and the vast emptiness of indecision, contrast, contradiction, and choice. We are the very things we want to avoid, and at the same time we are demanding the experience. It is in the very aspects of our contrasts, creativeness, and contradictions that we find authenticity, veracity, and outcomes from the activated soul. It is in the acceptance that all we are, all that brought us to this moment, brings us to a place of beauty where we can state with perfect clarity, the very words, "I am, because I simply am ..." What a simple and yet titillating answer to a question that comes to all of us, if we allow, embrace, and accept the authenticity of our soul.[5]

Note: At this time, it is illegal to possess, manufacture, and/or distribute Bofu medicine and many other plant medicines in many places, including the United States. It is recommended that one seek such experiences in areas where legalities are not an issue or the substances are not regulated. San Pedro, though technically illegal to consume as a medicine in the United States, is found growing across the country in yards, homes, and deserts.

[5]https://entheonation.com/blog/category/plant-medicines/san-pedro/

#1 International Best Selling author, Julia Irene Caton, made the connection between her heart, mind, and soul that led her on a journey to pursue her truth and attain a meaningful and fulfilling purpose in life. By accepting and surrendering to the teachers found in the darkness, she is able to embrace and accept the precious Light. Heart-Centered Therapeutic Coaching and Ministry was birthed as a modality to assist others in healing, accepting their own truths, and finding wholeness of being. Cohost to two different podcasts, *The Coached Soul* and *Real Talk with Julia and Lauren*, Julia is in the process of creating her own series entitled *The Heart of Healing, Health, and Habits*. She is the proud mother of five adult children and is a new Grammy J to her grandson, Caspian. Julia has an undergraduate degree in Human Development, a graduate degree in Human Relations with a focus on clinical mental health, and more than ten years' experience focusing on mental health, wellbeing, spiritual guidance and chaplancy. She currently offers Therapeutic Coaching, spiritual guidance, Transformation Tissue Therapy, TRUST Processing and Master level Reiki.

www.facebook.com/juliairenecaton
heartcenteredtherapeuticcoach@gmail.com
www.tiktok.com/@juliaiparks?_t=8WFpQh85C8J&_r=1

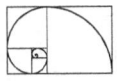

Jose Badillo

One More Second Chance

"Don't throw my baby out the window!" my mom yelled.
It was 1983, and I, at twenty-five days old,
was being held out a two-story window by my drunken father.

It's interesting how the universe, God, or however you'd like to put it, gives us life without the ability to fend for ourselves. Babies simply "be" and rely on whoever is around them. After the window event, I was with my mom for the first eight years of my life. She was all I knew, my everything. She went through many marriages, first with the father of my two older siblings, then my father, and then the father of my younger brother. Witnessing what a woman goes through on her own with children and life's challenges has molded me into being respectful and understanding of what a woman is worth. As a young boy who grew up without a father, I also understand how difficult it is to find strength, guidance, and the ability to feel aligned as we go through life's ups and downs. We learn many lessons confronting the obstacles and challenges in life. We don't need to know why things happen; they just do. It's part of life. It's up to us to learn how to navigate these challenges, keep our minds open to lessons learned, and discover the possibilities that can come from each situation.

At the age of seven, I remember my mom graduating from college as a computer technician and getting hired at a tech company in Silicon Valley. She brought home one of the very first computers she had built with video games on a floppy disc! We had a beautiful home with my older siblings and younger brother Diego. Life was looking so much better than how it started. But then yet another challenge arose, and my mom struggled with marriage issues that eventually saw her separated once again and my younger brother suddenly taken by his father to Mexico. Soon my mom became unemployed for passing out on the job due to stress. She couldn't handle losing her youngest son. We soon became homeless, and I can recall sleeping in the car with my mom.

One day she told me, "Son, it's time you live with Grandma for a while." Before taking me to Grandma's, she took me to see my father after bribing him for money to allow him to see me. I was happy to meet my father, but he was still having issues of his own.

It's difficult to find positive lessons when we're in survival mode. I've learned that if we can step out of ourselves, slow down and analyze with gratitude what we do have, then we can find a reason for pushing on and moving forward toward something better.

I lived with Grandma and family for a few years and became a really good Mexican folkloric dancer, performing on stage with some of the best mariachi bands, dancing in Cinco de Mayo parades, and was even on TV shows. Again, life was looking optimistic until Grandma returned me to my mom around eleven. When I went back to live with my mother, she was now a full-blown alcoholic living in a party house, which meant I had to adapt to a completely different lifestyle once again.

By then I was old enough to ask if life was trying to destroy me. I didn't feel life was on my side, or that I was meant to have it good; but deep down inside, I also knew those thoughts wouldn't serve me. I remember the day, at eleven years old, my older sister and brother dressed me up like them, gangsters, and took me out for a night on the town! We hung out on street corners with kids older than me looking for fun, drugs, and any people we could call "family."

I'll never forget the thought I had. "What am I doing here? Do I even belong?" Life truly felt like a roller coaster ride, and I was on the scariest ride ever! Not long after, I fell victim to the "hood" and got involved in drugs, gang fights, and crime, which eventually led to my incarceration. By the age of fifteen, I had a criminal record and was facing years in adult prison. I was only fifteen! Was I a lost cause? I knew inside I had more to give. I knew I needed to find a way out of my literal and symbolic confinement.

With the luck of God, I was freed at the age of eighteen. I had no idea what would become of me. I hung out with the wrong people and I struggled trying to stay off drugs. Then I met the mother of my now two children. I was twenty-one when my daughter was born, and though I had no career or idea what I wanted to do with my life, I had a burning desire to find a way forward. I wanted to create a magical life for myself, my family, and especially my daughter. I had a purpose and was working hard toward building a home and foundation for a better future.

Until one day, the mother of my daughter unexpectedly decided to leave me for someone else! Little did I know that after buying our first decent car, the car dealer would latch onto my beautiful fiancée. Again, I found myself asking if I wasn't worthy of the great life I was dreaming about. Why wasn't I enough?

Instead of giving up, I used the pain and suffering of my loss to find a way to succeed by knocking on every door, asking for help. I was determined to find a way to get my daughter back and build that vision I had.

Have you known that feeling, the one that makes you *freeze up, hold back, or push forward*? That's the basis of this story: my intuition that in spite of loss, pain, and obstacles, I knew I wasn't going to quit. I chose to keep on pushing until the day I landed a part-time job in a temp agency serving tables and washing dishes. I worked hard so that I could land a full-time job, which I did. It didn't take long before I was working my way up the ladder from a catering attendant, to catering director, to general manager and food service director of a high-tech company in

Silicon Valley. Me, Jose, worthy of a title as a director managing multimillion-dollar contracts and operations.

I was eventually able to reunite with my daughter and win back her mother, and we had our son. I was able to create a family and build a lifestyle I had never thought possible. I would love to say it was all good from there, but let's just say things happened and I became single once again. This time I was stronger, smarter, more determined than ever to face any challenges because the purpose of my children and my dreams and desires I worked on for so many years was stronger than any challenge or obstacle that got in my way.

The end of the story is I now live with my two children, own the temp staffing agency where I begged for a job, life coach others, and contribute back to the world. Things happened that I never could have imagined. When I stop and ask how or why, I realize it was the lessons I learned from hardship that got me where I am, made me who I am.

What does it take to find our balance and feel aligned with life? That's the biggest and best question I can present to you. We all go through struggles, and if we look at them the right way, we can see we are truly meant for more. Perhaps we weren't taught the "right" way. Maybe social media and our environment make us see and feel that we don't have all it takes or that we are not worthy. Maybe the challenges in life create confusion and make us question whether we can achieve something better for ourselves. However, we can go online, read books, or listen to people to confirm that the greatest achievers had many obstacles and challenges. They all had to push through when many others wouldn't dare! The majority of folks always end up wondering, "What could have been…if only I *would have, should have, hadn't* let that obstacle get in the way." Only after pushing forward no matter what, only after going through the clouds of pain and fear, can we come out on the other side. It's there that we can see the light, find a sense of calm and balance, then ultimately align with our true self.

As I look back, I ask what was it that helped me survive. What kept me pushing forward and not giving up. I believe in our spirit, heart, and soul (not our mind) that we know who we truly are. If we have more in us, then give it a go. Do not sit still. Life is energy, and we must use the energy in our body to first believe in ourselves, then clear our mind and feed it with possibility instead of doubt. We must look for answers with knowledge that's all around us that can give us ideas, clues, and opportunity. We must connect with those around us who can help us on our journey, and stay away from those who pull us down. If we can feed our body with energy, feed our mind with positive knowledge, connect with our deeper spirit and self, and surround ourselves with those whom we wish to be like, we can find our balance in life and continue to align with our purpose. There is endless opportunity for love and life at a deeper level, and, quite simply, we can never give up! We need to ask for yet another second chance. It's not what life gives us, but what we do with every second chance that matters.

Jose Badillo is a business owner, entrepreneur, and life coach. He has more than fifteen years of corporate dining and hospitality experience, working first as Catering Director, then advancing to Food Service Director managing corporate restaurant contracts for organizations such as Amazon, Ericsson, Federal Reserve Bank of San Francisco, and many others. He now works full time as President and CEO of his own hospitality staffing agency, providing jobs and service for corporate dining clients. Jose loves working as a life coach, sharing his ideas and inspiration to help others overcome many of life's obstacles. A graduate of Silicon Valley's Latino Board Leadership Academy, he has a passionate desire to give back to his community, and as a board member for the nonprofit organization New Voices for Youth, he helps young people find their voice and passions for the future. Finally, as a father of two, he now spends time investing in and studying real estate with his eighteen-year-old daughter. His passion is to live life to its fullest, always looking forward to new opportunities and never looking back, confident that it is what we do with the life we are given that matters most.

www.facebook.com/jose.badillo.503/
secondchancetolife.com
www.linkedin.com/in/jose-badillo-959b36135

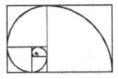

Precious Smith

From Misery to Joy

I appreciate how the Universe sends things my way to challenge the very essence of my thought processes! I have had so many of these experiences, and I appreciate each one of them. This time it was looking on the internet to locate the dictionary definition of the word *alignment*. Defined, alignment means to bring into a line. That was clearly not helping me. I then looked up the word *align*. Align means to bring into cooperation or agreement with a particular group, party, cause, etcetera. OK, stay with me! *To bring into cooperation or agreement*. I am not going to focus on a group, party, or a cause. I am focusing on bringing myself into agreement with myself.

I was once four hundred pounds. I was miserable in every way imaginable. I put on a smile for all occasions because everyone wanted to be around the jolly woman with the big personality. I used to wonder just how people could be in my presence when I did not want to be in my own presence. I was in a marriage that left me feeling unfulfilled and unloved. In 2014, my youngest child was born. It was decided that I would stay home with her and not work. I filled my days with naps, cleaning, mothering, food, and more food! I was not working, which was one of the few times in my life I did not have an income, so I did not have my own finances to take care of myself.

I remember, once, needing a new tire. I was so afraid to tell my spouse at the time that I needed something. I felt as if I burdened her. I phoned a friend who took me to a used-tire place, and I used the last of the money that was in my bank account to purchase a tire for my car. I was broke. I did not qualify for any financial assistance because I was married. I did not have any other backup money in my bank account because I had just purchased a tire. The only money my partner would spend was either on the baby or groceries. So, what did I end up doing in my hours and times of boredom? I went into the kitchen and cooked entire soul-food meals—daily. I followed that up by *eating* entire soul-food meals every day. I gained more than seventy-five pounds following the birth of my daughter. I dieted. I tried to exercise. I tried to be more mobile. I tried to not eat at all. None of it seemed to work. Nothing! I continued to get bigger.

I was told, "You are not too big, but you are getting pretty close. When your weight gets to be too much, I will let you know!" I was hurt. Here I was taking care of my child every day and thinking that I was living my life. I was brought back to Earth with the chilling discovery that my survival in life was dependent on another person. I would not have a place to lay my head if I became too big for my partner. I lost it. I became depressed. My anxiety went through the ceiling. I stopped existing! I only took care of my child and my oldest daughter; other than that, I was in the house. This was pre-pandemic. It was during a time when one could go outside and not have to worry about a mask. (Actually, I preferred to stay at home. There are so many germs out there!)

Fast-forward to 2016. I had weight-loss surgery. To qualify I had to have a psychological evaluation for my insurance. I instantly began to worry. My mental health had severely declined. It had to have been divine intervention that allowed me to pass that hurdle. I learned during this phase that I also had sleep apnea, prediabetes, and high blood pressure. I felt like I wanted to give up on life in general. The only thing that kept this momma going was my daughters. If I was unable to get my shit together, my children were going to lose me! So I asked the Universe to allow me a healthier option where my heart, mind, job, and life could be at peace. I indeed qualified through my insurance to have weight-loss surgery. That's when my healing myself began so that I could present the best form of myself.

I realized that no form of outside influence should have such control over me that I am unable to do things that truly bring me abundant joy. First, I had to figure out what things truly bring me joy. Me! Then I had to teach myself that it was alright to take space and have boundaries. It was alright to say no! It was alright to be able to have downtime. It was alright to not help a person if I was mentally in a space where my cup was empty. At one point, I felt like I was being so selfish, and as if I were stealing from myself by making myself a priority—both at the same time. I had never prioritized myself this way.

And yet every time I said no to something that did not bring me joy, I felt like I was finding a piece of my life that had been stolen. I collected those pieces and put together *Precious 2.0*. I'd managed to balance myself. I was in a space where I could receive love. I was also in a space where I was ready to pursue next steps to create a better me. Realizing that I was worth all the pomp and circumstance that it would take to get beyond the walls that trauma had built was absolutely priceless! I began blogging. Findingmyselfat40.com has been a lifesaver. I was able to put my thoughts onto paper so that I could create realizations for myself.

I went back to work in 2015. I absolutely love teaching students. I feel rewarded having the privilege of teaching young minds. Occasionally, it gets frustrating, but it is the best career that I could have chosen for myself. I worked through my own crap, and it took more than four years to get myself to a level where I was at peace.

Currently, I live my life at a level I could only have dreamed about seven years ago. I have an amazing job. I got divorced. I settled into a semi-amicable custody agreement with my ex. My oldest daughter is a senior in college. She is an independent, loving, kind, and beautiful soul. My youngest daughter is the extroverted diva that I expected her to be. I married a woman who I met eighteen years ago (the Universe has a sense of humor). She, along with my daughters, keep me on task. We bought a house that we affectionately named P and S Homestead. We have a yard big enough to have a garden, fruit trees, animals, and our home. It is the home and yard of my dreams. I got a raise! Teachers will never be paid enough for the amazing work that they do with their students, but I was able to pay off my credit cards. I just received an email from my credit monitoring service that said many of my student loans were paid off. OK, Universe, I see you working it out in my favor. Let me add that I have been blessed to lose half of myself since 2016. I currently weigh less than two hundred pounds. I am a sexy wife! I am so fortunate to be in this space. I worked like a crazy woman to get here. I put in the work! I was sent exactly what I needed when I thought I would lose my shit. I believe now that all will be well. There will undoubtedly be times when things get a little hairy, but those, too, shall pass.

My life has transitioned one hundred and eighty degrees since my depression and anxiety in 2015. I got the help that I needed to put me onto a path of happiness. The work was the most painful, enlightening, amazing, hurtful, and cleansing endeavor of my life. When I was going through it, I dreamed of being in the space where I am now. Homeownership, great marriage, healthy kids, an amicable custody space, a fun career, and meaningful people in my life help me keep it all together. I am now the woman of my dreams. I have aligned my mind, spirit, body, and finances. I am in agreement with myself. Oh, what joy I have found during this season of alignment!

Precious Smith is a Black lesbian, wife, mother, activist, advocate, teacher, sister, daughter, and friend! She carries all these titles proudly and with adoration for every person who is a part of her human experience. Precious has been a teacher for nine years and a homeowner for less than a year. She teaches at a middle school in a very family-oriented neighborhood. The children she teaches, including her two daughters, are the highlights of why she is who she is. They have inspired Precious to be the best version of herself available. Her amazing wife's name is Stephanie. She has been exceptional in helping Precious realize that she is more than enough! No matter how many times she was told that she was enough, it didn't matter until Stephanie's actions helped her realize that she is enough. She has done the work, and her family has been with her through it all. Now she teaches children to genuinely be who they are—authentically, unapologetically, and always.

www.findingmyselfat40.com/
www.facebook.com/precious.smith/
www.pandshomestead.com/

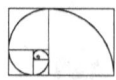

Anonymous V

V for Veronica

I thought of Megan recently. Megan was my disabled brother's nanny, one of his favorites. We let her go because of a methamphetamine habit she could not beat despite my mother's expertise in addiction/recovery and offer to take her in. Sadly, she passed away from her addiction about a year later.

I thought of her in a positive light with good memories. I felt myself wanting to talk to Megan the way that I have spoken to Veronica and other souls who have kept me company throughout my life. They are my friends, although they have gone quiet lately. I find myself lonely without them in a way I cannot explain.

I wished I could speak to Megan right then.

Suddenly, I heard her say hi, and I said hi back, and she was almost surprised by the fact that I could hear her. "Wait, do you actually understand everything I'm saying to you?" she asked.

I was like, "Yeah, or at least I feel that I do."

She went on, "Because something very strange happened right before we started talking to each other." She described her desire to speak to me and her experience, that she was wherever she was but could tell something was coming from behind her, so she turned and saw waves of light. Light waves of all the same color were coming from one source, like a pebble thrown into the middle of a pond. She knew it wasn't just coming toward her; it was coming and going in every direction away from and toward wherever it originated. She realized it was seeking her. It started getting dimmer as it approached the area around her. Things got brighter the instant it touched her, and then the whole wave started going back in on itself. It was imploding, but the area of light around her wasn't leaving. It was showing her the way to whatever just came.

"It wasn't doing this for any of the others, so I knew it was looking for me," she said. "I felt a positive energy. It felt like an old friend trying to get my attention. I followed it all the way back to where you were. There was so much light releasing into me from what you had done. I couldn't tell it was you yet. It was just bright around you, but eventually I knew I was at the source of the light. And when I saw *you*, I was like, 'Wow, that is not what I was expecting!'"

She had a surprised voice. I remember it now. You know the kind of surprised sound like an old friend surprised to see you? Then, there was her realization that I could hear her! The conversation didn't start with her telling me what it was like for her, though.

It started out, "Well, hi." I said "hey," and then she replied like a normal conversation. She was expecting to reply and not be heard, since that is how it usually went. "But this time, instead of 'Oh Megan, I miss you! I wish you were here' or something like that, you could hear me."

"I was just remembering and thinking of you, Megan."

She said, "Wait, can you hear me?"

"Yeah, I guess you didn't know that I can hear spirits." I didn't really know if it was true either, but I could feel that I heard her. So, perhaps?

She asked, "You need help with this?"

I said, "Hell yeah!" And that's when she told me all about how she found me with energy light. I was thinking about Megan in a positive way, and I heard her in my head the same way I have heard Veronica my whole life. Megan said it's because at some point the positive thinking and my gifts innately aligned with her energy and called to her.

I sensed she felt happy where she was. I got no impression she needed me to free her from anything. I sensed she had people to hang out with.

She's been doing her own thing for a while. I hadn't thought about her intensely lately, for whatever reason, but that day it was enough to get her attention (very clearly, apparently). She wanted very much to go to that light.

She described the event like watching the brightest light on a weld arc as it slowly faded. She was like, "Hey, that caught my attention. I'm gonna go there because something is telling me, 'Hey, you should come over here. You know nothing bad is going on.'" When she got there, she saw it was me and so she said hi and thought "Something's about to happen." And then it did.

I thought, "Obviously she's right."

She said, "I didn't know you could do this!"

"I didn't know for sure I could either," I said, "but we're both here."

"So you're questioning your sanity because this is not the normal thing we're taught in school?" she asked.

"Yes, I am questioning! I constantly question if this is even possible or if I'm crazy." I wouldn't say I believe, but I like to think it's true. If it's true, it lets me hear Veronica—or is she my imagination too? This is my dilemma, the problem, the confusion, the misalignment. I don't know what I believe. My mentor says if I would allow myself to communicate with them more, I could do more with my gifts and understand them better. She always recommends that I meditate, meditate, meditate.

Sometimes the inflow of others' energy is too much, so I close off completely. This also closes me off from Veronica and the others I enjoy. I experience a loneliness I don't have words for. I am detached. I miss them and want to align with them again. But I want to open the door, not the floodgates.

This would be an excellent time to start meditating. Megan may have made me hear her, but if I had to give credit to anybody for this, it would be Veronica. She has been on me about this for years now. Speaking to Megan made me open to hearing them again. She showed me the value and benefits in being aligned with my gifts: the sense of connection! I've decided to make time to work this muscle the way I have decided to work my physical muscles at the gym. Meditate.

I remembered Megan how I last saw her, at the end. She gently tried to show me how she looks now, but not very hard. She wanted me to see her happy.

Then Veronica came, and I felt my tears welling up and a smile forming on my face. She wanted me to meditate. I missed our conversations. People need to meditate. Veronica repeats this every time I ask if she has anything else she would like to share.

I believe I simply have a desire for connection. Sometimes I feel like I've already lost my gifts to communicate. Then, for a moment, there they are. These energies have helped me deal with some of the bad things I've experienced in life. I have missed Veronica's company, having her presence. I'm grateful I haven't completely lost it; I just know I don't have it *in* me. I don't feel her as I had previously. She was trying to make contact, and there were days when it was harder than others to hear her. I've felt a need to open again so that when I need her it isn't so hard to find her. Once it becomes even slightly hard for me to locate her, it causes an immediate anxiety of, "Fuck, well this is another great part of my life that's not real," or believing I've just been a lunatic all along.

I don't want to be put on any sort of medication. No one has ever said that it felt good. I knew there was a need for meditation, but instead I said, "I'm sure I need to *meditate* more, but if there's any other fucking thing I can do, please give it to me." I can't even remember why I had that thought, but a few days later I heard from Megan.

I think we all have gifts, but perhaps we do not always listen to them. We do not always align with them. Alignment is knowing that I know who these beings are when I hear them. That's *my* gift. I receive comfort and protection in their friendship. Sometimes I know why they call to me, but often not. This is a place I find peace even in the least peaceful of times. It is my relationship with these gifts that has helped me make it this far in this body. The mental illness label was given to me by others. The gifts come from the Light and the voices.

We, all of us, need to meditate more. Meditate more, meditate more. Veronica says so.

V for Veronica.

▼ ▼ ▼ ▼ ▼

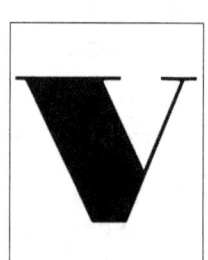

"Cooper" is an anonymous author who communicates with souls who are at the point of passing. A few of these souls have befriended him for life. He is a medium. Years in a mental health setting that did not accept these gifts led to him to an adolescent and early adulthood of depression and imagined psychosis.

Cooper's precious abilities to communicate with those who have passed has been a gift he has had his whole life, and a struggle he still battles to understand. He has only recently come into alignment with the blessing that his connection to these heightened senses can be for a human. He is fascinated by the abilities of the brain and would like any gifts in the form of donation to go to finding a cure for ALS, the disease that took one of the greatest human minds, Stephen Hawking.

www.als.org/
Addiction? Please call 1-800-254-4070 for all the Megans who didn't.
www.samhsa.gov

"Alignment is
never achieved,
it is a space best
danced within."

— Mistilei

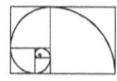

Bethany Pitchford

The Deepest Blue

Well, then it is as you please. This is the dysfunction talking.
This is the disease talking. This is how much I miss you talking.
This is the deepest blue, talking, talking, always talking to you.

–Maggie Nelson, Bluets

It started on a normal west Texas Saturday in August.

It ended after sixty-four minutes of gun shots left seven people dead, twenty-one others injured, and many more dealing with secondary trauma.

But did the trauma really end?

It's over for him, he had his sixty-four minutes of fame. Most of them get six minutes. Most shootings are over in six minutes.

360 seconds.

But he had 3,840 seconds.

For 3,840 seconds, I wondered if all of my friends and family were safe. But it still didn't end.

There are 31,556,952 seconds in a year. I have been fighting to find any sense of safety, justice, and recovery for 31,556,952 seconds and counting…

Does trauma ever really end?

Because you see, the blue started out subtle, like a gentle ocean, rolling up on the beach, when the sky-high anxiety level transformed into panic attacks.

I start shaking. It's harder to breathe. I'm a goldfish being watched. I want to run away, but I can't because I'm frozen. I'm stuck. I'm scared. I'm silent. I'm screaming. All my thoughts start swirling and swirling and swirling until I can't concentrate on one. Then come the tears and gasping for air. And the waiting for it to pass. And the exhaustion after. It wasn't really about that midterm, people.

Does trauma ever really end?

Because, you see, the blue of the ocean no longer looks gentle on the beach. I am looking into the darkest depths as the panic transforms into depression. Getting out of bed is almost impossible. I just want to sleep for a really long time—it's the only place that's really safe, locked in here, in the quiet, under my weighted blanket, alone.

Day in and day out I try to keep up the routine, the façade, pretending that I really am doing better, because they're all expecting me to be doing better—some of them have even said so.

"Do you want to try this on and see if you'd be doing better by now?"

Yeah, I didn't think so.

So here I am, out in the ocean, on this boat, all alone, watching the whales. Eyeballs above water!

Does trauma ever really end?

Then came the moment I could see the surface again—the moment when a mentor said "You're in the middle of a mental illness struggle. This isn't your fault. We're going to get you through this." I'll never forget that moment. I didn't know how I would end up being okay. But I knew I would be okay.

And then, so many of the people in my tribe came and sat on that tiny boat with me in the middle of the ocean until I found my way back to shore:

I want to see you do well. No, I want to see you be well.

People that you've confided in see a stronger more self-assured you who advocates for the things she needs.

I believe you will be okay. One rough semester doesn't make you a bad teacher.

We're right here, always.

Come over and study with me. You don't have to do it alone.

I am here whenever you need me.

I care about your well-being.

Just know I'm here for you.

You just focus on you right now. I can handle teaching this class.

Your illness is not your identity. Your chemistry is not your character.

If you don't exhale eventually, you'll pop.

Hope. Always hope.

Take a deep breath, get back in there, and stay in the fight.

I'm here. And I'm here to tell you it does get better.

They stayed with me and supported me until I found my way again.

Does trauma ever really end?

No, no it doesn't.

I will always carry it.

But it does get better.

Together, we will rise.

Together, we did rise.

Together, we shattered stigma.

Together, we made it to recovery.

Now, it's three years later.

Now, I understand secondary trauma is real.

Now, I see my mental health struggles are not my fault.

Now, I understand that recovery is a journey and not a destination.

Does trauma ever really end?

No, no it doesn't.

I will always carry it.

But it does get better.

Now, there are days where, with enough hard work, the tea, and the right playlist, I feel unstoppable. There are days where I'm genuinely in my joy and my power without overthinking it, such as when I'm teaching my advertising writing class and watching my students' creativity grow.

But there are still things I must carry every day, such as the fear of losing my people. Sometimes, the fear of losing one of them still hits me out of nowhere, like a surprise ocean wave making its way over the side of our tiny yellow boat, threatening to drown us if we don't start swimming fast. There are still days when I'm down. There are still days when I'm anxious. There are still days when I have panic attacks. There are even still days when I need mental health medication just to make it through.

But one thing remains true—I know I'm not alone. The people in my tribe are the reason I made it through the hardest semester of my life. The people in my tribe are the reason I've found joy again during recovery. And I'm grateful for each of them.

You see, the thing about hope is that it's a renewable resource. And where there is hope, there is power, recovery, and healing.

So, for anyone out there reading this story and feeling hopeless, don't give up. It's okay to not be okay. It's okay to reach out and ask for help. It's okay to take the first step toward recovery.

You are never alone.

Bethany Pitchford is a Ph.D. student in the College of Media and Communication at Texas Tech University (TTU). Her research interests include how creativity helps people cope with mental illness and how mental illness is portrayed in news stories when journalists report on mass shootings. She graduated with her master's in Mass Communication from Texas Tech after earning her bachelor's degree in Technical Communication from TTU, and she received her Associate of Science degree with a major in Biology from Midland College. She enjoys serving on the executive board for Healing in the Arts, a TTU organization where students tell their stories via creative media in order to begin the healing process. In her spare time, she enjoys creative writing, painting, photography, yoga, and taking care of her plants.

www.youtube.com/watch?v=QaIVUlVb5fM
www.bethpitchford17@gmail.com.
www.facebook.com/media/set/?set=a.500747473315856&type=3
www.linkedin.com/in/bethanypitchford
scholar.google.com/citations?hl=en&user=MnxLGvAAAAAJ

If you or someone you know need help, you can contact the National Alliance on Mental Illness (NAMI) HelpLine. The NAMI HelpLine can be reached Monday through Friday, 10 a.m.–10 p.m., ET. Call 1-800-950-NAMI (6264), text "HelpLine" to 62640 or email us at helpline@nami.org.

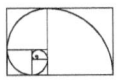

Kelly Hanna

It's Time to Remember

Who the F You Are

I could write volumes on my personal journey. From skydiving and wing walking before birth; growing up with a mother who was a poster child for generational trauma; learning how to take care of a newborn starting at age six; picking corn in the summers; then packing up my little Toyota Corolla and moving across the country from Wisconsin to Florida. I could write about the man who raised me, a military police officer in Vietnam and a career law enforcement officer, whose influence and expectation of perfection actually turned into a tremendous blessing and gifts that have taken me far in life. I've gone from growing up in a very unhealthy family to becoming a raw-food vegan passionately pursuing an insatiable hunger to understand what true health means to the body, the mind, and the soul.

I was completely clueless about what self-discovery even looked like as I floated through life, having no idea who I was, what I wanted, or that I was even allowed to have dreams. That journey took me to being in a marriage that blessed me with two incredible daughters but turned into a decade of experiencing someone at war with themselves, controlled by multiple addictions. This led me to being widowed when I was thirty-eight years old.

Still not knowing who I was led me to another toxic relationship that further damaged both my daughters and myself. Having no idea how to have a relationship with myself, I was full throttle in survival mode, reactive and believing my life was doomed to emotional pain and misery.

Somehow, as a result of a series of miracles and miraculous human beings along the way, I managed to keep believing there was a better way, a better path, a better me. One of those miracles was a complete stranger gifting me a ticket to a Tony Robbins event where the mission to finding "me" became nonnegotiable. Where I sobbed (and sobbed) and began the first steps to being clear about who I am, who I craved to be, and all I wanted to create.

Finally aware of my generational trauma, I put my flag in the ground: *it ends with me*. I vowed to heal for my daughters, for their children and their children's children. I vowed to heal for myself and all the lives I wanted to be able to touch who just might need a nudge into believing they, too, could discover they are a valuable, miraculous human being who has a higher purpose.

Now let me be very, *very* clear: this journey included bumps, bruises, every emotion known to humanity, highs, lows, devastation, and endless tests of my sanity. However, it was within the darkest moments, the messiest of messes, that I found the stillness, the clarity, the tenacity, and the resilience to keep putting one foot in front of the other. The harder I fell or got knocked down, the more determined I was to rise.

What did I learn? I learned that love is *always* the answer, but it starts from the inside out. You and you alone must love yourself first. Your initial core values around that will form the blueprints you carry with you into adulthood and every single relationship moving forward.

At a very young age, we are groomed to believe we have to sacrifice ourselves, and our view of self-love gets horribly distorted. But here is the truth: you write the story! You and you alone are at the helm of your life. No one, and I mean no one, can take your joy, happiness, or hope without your permission. This is your cue to stop giving those things away, to stop giving yourself away. It starts with awareness. Awareness is powerful beyond measure. So is action. How many people get completely lost wasting their precious time waiting and procrastinating, frozen in fear and terrified of uncertainty? Too many!

I equate finding alignment to finding out you actually have *abs*. It can be a painful discovery—one you may believe will only come with unbelievable endurance and suffering. You try a little bit of everything to build those abs. Once you have them, you are so proud! You can't stop looking at them in the mirror. You want to show them off everywhere you go. Then you realize they were there all along and that the only reason you lost them was because you were distracted and misdirected.

Finding alignment is simply learning how to find your way home. Quiet the "wet cats on acid" that keep your mind spinning in a million directions at once, the inner dialogue that keeps your light far too dim, that causes you to doubt everything and to believe that you're not worth anything, then to feel surprised, hurt, and wounded when the world doesn't value you either. That overthinking brain you somehow learned to believe was your voice is false. Nothing could be further from the truth. You must believe that the answers are within.

Far too many people spend their entire lifetime seeking happiness and truth in their external environment. I could quote Tony Robbins 24/7. I have dozens of journals from twelve years of going to more events than I can count and volunteering hundreds of hours of my time supporting his events. I had to be in that room. It was my oxygen—soul nourishment— at a level I could never describe. I have to clarify here, it wasn't just the content. It was (and continues to be) the people I have met in the environment. The movers, the shakers, the doers. The people who commit to a higher purpose, who have done the work to peel back the layers of who they are and what they want. I am blessed to be surrounded by people who live their lives with true passion. People whose priorities are to serve, contribute, learn, and never tire of growth.

You must live life *forward*. Honor the good, the bad, and the ugly as opportunities and blessings. Find people who have learned to make fear their bitch. People who love to feel alive. People who aren't afraid to call you out with tremendous love in the name of growth and expansion. People who hold space for you to process and evolve with no judgment. Believe with all your heart that the universe doesn't make mistakes. Believe with every cell in your being that life is happening *for you, not to you*. Every time I am faced with something that challenges me, I literally say those words in my head over and over.

Does that mean if you put in the work life becomes beautiful and perfect? Absolutely not. In fact, just one week before I was invited to be a part of this publication, I unexpectedly and tragically lost my love of seven years, a person who truly accepted and loved *all* of me, who taught me what it means to be loved unconditionally. But when you take the time to put the work in, it equips you to be able to stay grounded, and challenges you to up-level and take you places beyond your wildest dreams. The coolest part is that your dreams get bigger and bigger! Once you can see what can be done, it becomes what *must* be done.

The first question I ask, and one that completely perplexes people, is: "Who are you and what do you really want?" Yes, I am *that* person who bypasses superficial conversation and starts asking deep, purposeful questions. Yes, I get met with eye rolls and awkwardness. Someone in my own family told me I am just plain "batshit crazy." I don't mind being misunderstood. My hope is that you get curious. That you see a glimmer of light within yourself that craves to burn brighter.

Someone once told me that we are one big radio tower. Every morning and every moment throughout the day, you get to choose what you dial into. This needs to be done with clarity and intention. What "frequencies" do you want to attract? Are you clear on *what you want to manifest*? Are you clear on what you *don't* want to attract? Are you attaching excitement and emotion to those thoughts? Ask yourself what you want to be in alignment with.

The universe is waiting to respond; it simply needs your direction, whether it is conscious or not. Visualize yourself walking through the most amazing mansion you have ever seen. Behind every door is a room filled to the brim with miracles and gifts, yet you wander the hallways lost. Start opening the doors! A dear friend and the head of a group I belong to lives by the mantra "Be a magic moment millionaire." I strongly encourage you to do the same. The universe did not make a mistake bringing you into existence. Start acting like the miracle you are. Start approaching life with playful curiosity and rapturous anticipation. It's time to remember who the F you are! Welcome home.

Kelly Hanna is a leader, mentor, public speaker, published author, and expert in advertising, video production, social media, and business growth and development, with over three decades of experience in PR, advertising, and branding, two decades of Emmy award winning television and video production, and more than a decade of graphic design and social media. A nationally published photographer, internationally published blogger specializing in Caribbean travel, and certified Google guide, she's spent more than a decade immersed in personal development. Kelly has traveled the globe interviewing hundreds of celebrities and leaders, and has had the privilege of capturing and telling the stories of incredible humans, heroes, and places. Kelly single-handedly built her first million-dollar business at twenty-eight and her second after being widowed at thirty-eight while raising her two young daughters. Kelly also has a tremendous passion for functional and integrative medicine. She sits on the board of the nonprofit Live to Give. She is an incredibly proud mom and currently resides in South Florida.

www.facebook.com/Cat5Kelly
www.instagram.com/kellyhannavideo/
www.linkedin.com/in/kellyhannavideopro-human-and-brand-poten-tialstrategist-and-speaker-49a146a/
www.bigsproutmedia.com

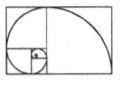

Kym Luck

15-Love

As a shy, yet cheeky child, my needs were simple. Warm summer days in Wisconsin, a few cartoons, some cereal, weekends with Dad and Grandma watching Disney, picking vegetables out of Aunt Pat's garden, exploring the creek, playtime with cousins, picking up stray dogs, and spending time on horses that my aunts taught me to ride. A day alone riding in the country on a horse named Bert, butterflies fluttering on my skin, and outstretched arms caressing the cornstalks gave me great happiness. Joy was my general state of being.

Outside forces hit me hard in my ninth year. It was as if my life became a game of tennis. The net was where I was my most joyful, authentic self, but outside forces volleyed me back and forth, sometimes near the net and other times way out of bounds. Each side of the net presented extreme challenges, and I often found myself sad and lonely.

My parents divorced. Siblings were born. Two village-idiot stepparents joined "the family" with their children. We moved out of state, away from my dad, grandma, and cousins; it was agonizing. Between kindergarten and twelfth grade, I attended ten schools in seven cities in five states. I majored in making friends again and again. Four days after high school graduation in Texas, we moved to California because my fear-driven mom didn't want me to go to University of Texas at Austin because it took me too far away from her. I attended junior college outside of Sacramento for one year and then Sacramento State for one semester. I wanted to be a marine biologist, but Enlightened Village Idiot #1 said,

"There's no money in that!" It was difficult to feel excited about anything long term when living with closed-minded adults.

Until I was nineteen and things happened. One was Mom sending me on an errand to buy cigarettes. An older man drove up in his convertible Mercedes. I was easily wowed and thought, "I must be very mature to attract an older man." Of course, a thirty-six-year-old misogynistic narcissist would be attracted to a nineteen-year-old. Eight months into that relationship, after extensive grooming and systematic elimination of my friends and family, the old guy said, "You need to be punished." The first blows were brutally dealt via a tennis racket. As I type this, it is after using the analogy of my life becoming a tennis game. I digress. I didn't have anyone to call because, time and again, I had chosen him over them. He told me he would give up his singlehood if I could prove to him that I could have children. So I got pregnant. On purpose! And another ball was thrown into the court. I had two extreme emotional experiences happening simultaneously.

My son John was the brightest light in my life experience thus far. A curly-haired little cherub with deep, brown eyes, he was happy and easy. My heart was so full. He was also my supreme challenge as he grew older, being highly intelligent and active. When he was four and one-half, I got the courage to leave his father.

I was boiling with hatred and rage from enduring betrayal and emotional, verbal, and physical abuse. For an entire year I would go to bed each night, wondering if I could pour gas on my husband, light it and get away before he killed all three of us. Yes. I was pushed to that point. That kind of thought had never entered my mind prior to life with that man. I was, and still am, a very nice person, but I knew then I would not allow him or anyone to fuck with me again. It was time to take control of my game of tennis. When he left for work one day, I disappeared. Without a trace.

Three weeks after leaving, I reappeared, began divorce proceedings, and started going to school. My rent was $700, car payment $339, daycare $900, tuition, insurance…compared to $540 for child support. I had nine W-2s that first year. Whatever it took to make it, I did it. A few of those W-2 jobs and a degree led to my short career as a software engineer. My parents were happy.

Because it seemed like the right thing to do, I overcorrected, married a really nice guy and had two more beautiful, perfect children. We had the house, the dog, the yard, the trampoline. The job that made my parents so happy. Yea! I quit shortly after meeting a man with forty horses. For five years I was his intern and learned about large-herd management. We were living in Seattle at the time, and the weather was killing me. The house interior was painted no fewer than eight times as I looked for the happy color. The kids and I moved to Colorado while my husband continued working until the house sold. This was a move that put me on top of the net. I was filled with vitality and energy running a children's horse camp. After the house sold and he moved to Colorado, I became acutely aware of the dissonance in our relationship. So I got divorced, again.

The following year, my beautiful, precious, nineteen-year-old John was killed in an accident when another driver crossed the yellow line. I can't really remember much of the following three years. My old story and all the challenges I had experienced thus far seemed trivial, inconsequential. The net wasn't even visible. The moon was closer to it than I was.

Desperate to communicate with my other son, who felt invisible after the death of his older brother, I registered the two of us for a Tony Robbins *Unleash the Power Within* event, hoping we would reconnect. We developed a common language that empowered us, and we learned strategies to strengthen our minds and master our emotions. A distinction Tony made that helped me was, "The reason we grieve so hard is that we feel it shouldn't have happened." It gave me clarity and perspective on the human condition. We are all going to suffer unimaginable and difficult challenges. It's what we do in those times and the meaning we apply to those challenges that determine our future path. If we are seeking alignment with our truest, most authentic and joyful selves, we need to apply better meanings to those moments. I choose to create the life I want, not just manage it. I control my distance from the net.

A test of that control occurred in 2018 when my all-time best boyfriend of fourteen years and I executed our four-year plan and moved to Wyoming. The sale of my horse business in Colorado was nearly complete. It was all puppy dogs and rainbows! My daughter and I were in Iceland for her gap year when the text messages from my guy turned to gibberish. Upon my return to the United States, he abruptly and unceremoniously left me for a younger woman. I was homeless—both physically and in my heart. We had moved to a house in Wyoming owned by his uncle, so I couldn't tell him to move. When I asked him what I should do, he replied coldly, "Go to your sister's." I asked him if he had a brain tumor or if he had been abducted by aliens because this behavior was definitely new and shocking. Driving a truck and a trailer loaded with my stuff, I headed to dreary Seattle. Every song I listened to was a sad love song. When it was time to tell my son about the recent events, his response was, "Well, Mom, life is happening for you, not to you."

Damn you, Tony Robbins! I halted the sale of my business. I worked hard to redefine what "home" meant to me. I allowed thirty days of tears, and then I joined Tinder. My plan was to go on fifty first dates. To see who I was and who was out there. There were a lot of duds. Tony Robbins calls them knights who never grew up. There were also a lot of good guys. Each date was a small volley, a small lesson that helped me define the standards of my ideal intimate relationship. It all led to a realization that I don't need one to thrive.

The horseback riding business I nearly sold now has fifty-five horses. It makes *me* happy. My son and daughter work with me now and again, which gives me even more pleasure. When I ride in the mountains, on my favorite horse Meno, my arms stretch out wide and my fingers caress the leaves of aspen trees under blue summer skies. I *am* the net.

That very net, the one that is the best version of me so far, just caught an outstanding man from Indiana. He is someone I've known for thirteen years. He showed up to go hunting at my place last week, and I saw him with new eyes. I also learned he grew up ninety minutes away from my aunt's farm where I rode through the cornfields on my favorite horse Bert, with my arms stretched wide under blue summer skies. Today, with both my existence and my purpose in alignment, I keep my eye on the ball, the net in sight, my game in mind, and enter the court of life with confidence.

▼ ▼ ▼ ▼ ▼

Kym Luck earned her bachelor's in liberal studies from the University of Washington, which led to a job as a software engineer at the Microsoft campus. In 2003, she purchased Vail Stables in Vail, Colorado, where Kym offers scenic horseback rides, goat yoga, and G.O.A.T. Happy Hour. Her individual and team equine coaching helps people overcome their fears while building confidence and elevating their horsemanship skills. Her coaching also helps restore harmony to work groups through games and challenges using horses as a modality. Her nomadic life toggles between Colorado, Arizona, and Indonesia (for a good dive). She is the mother of two well-adjusted adults, a collector of amazing women friends, *the* favorite auntie, and her Corgi's girlfriend. No onions or coffee please.

www.facebook.com/kym.luck
whoiskympossible@gmail.com
vailstables.com/

"The idea of failure is silly.
You either succeed or
choose to stop.
As long as you remain in
alignment, failure is an
impossible idea."

— Mistilei

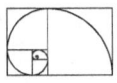

Oluwa Adams

Presence and Its Awakening Power

My mother told me I once came out of my room at a very young age with a look of joy and wonderment. I had seen a bright light that filled the entire room. While I was in college, I would suddenly become aware of the *inner self*, and I occasionally experienced being blissfully awake, even during deep sleep.

As time passed, many powerful spiritual awakening experiences revealed significant aspects of human existence that changed the course of my life. These experiences started aligning my own existence and the purpose for which I was born.

After meditating for many years and engaging in numerous healing modalities, I was happier than my earlier days, which had been filled with anger and depression.

Around 2010, I experienced massive existential stress. I began to feel a heavy sense of intense anguish, more than I had ever experienced. Nothing was working in my life. I had given up my dreams of a career in acting and music to pursue a PhD program in mythology, with emphasis in depth psychology. When I learned that my dissertation, *A Map of Consciousness*, wasn't going to be accepted by my supervisors, I felt frustrated and unhappy, although still determined to write about the topic closest to my heart. I wanted to stay true to that. Furthermore, two of my three core spiritual teachers, Leonard Jacobson and Bhagavan Ozen, pointed out that my deep desire to obtain the PhD was acting as an obstacle to my awakening.

I attended one of Leonard Jacobson's events and shared with him my frustration about my PhD dissertation. As I walked toward my seat, he looked at me with intense Buddha eyes and told me that he hoped I didn't get my PhD. This was shocking and upsetting, and yet I trusted that what he said had a deeper truth. Soon after, while meditating, Bhagavan Ozen appeared in my meditation and said the PhD had to go. This was clearly to prepare me for the subsequent events.

In 2012, after meditating, I had a sudden, massive explosion on my crown chakra. It was so loud it woke me up—energetically, spiritually, and physically. The explosion was so intense I found myself out of my body in a different dimension. As I looked around, I saw the infinite cosmos. There were stars everywhere, like grains of sand on the beach. I experienced the I AM THAT I AM, which everyone is. I experienced the sensation of trillions of whole-body orgasms at the same time. Words cannot describe being one with all of it. I looked beyond that dimension and saw the blackness, the galactic source from which the cosmos emanates. It took me a while to realize what had happened.

Previously, I was unaware that I could go back to the Source like this. I enjoyed the state I was in and began to feel more joyful and happier, more at ease in every situation, and things began bothering me less. I began experiencing the inner state of Being-ness, the I AM. All along, I thought it was going to happen differently, but I discovered that's not how it works. It is different for everyone. I was also aware that one doesn't have to be perfect to awaken.

This was my big misunderstanding. Awakening doesn't mean I am living in bliss all the time. Awakened, I can be in a state of unconditional peace while still experiencing emotional turmoil. I can awaken and then do the integration work, or I can engage in both simultaneously. For example, at the end of another relationship, it felt like I was experiencing "hell" while I was simultaneously experiencing unconditional peace.

There are many who are already awake; however, waiting to be perfect, they don't know it yet. Even after my first awakening I would often go in and out of the awakened state. I knew it hadn't fully integrated and that there was work to be done. I had to feel into my own heart space to heal the pain in my heart, which is a prerequisite for the integration and embodiment process.

Going to the depths of my emotional pain was bearable because the I AM Presence was/is already awake in me. I felt the pain of humanity and began to see part of the human struggle. We have all done things in our unconsciousness that have contributed to the suffering of humanity and this planet. Awakening happens differently for everyone through a process of allowing and sitting with one's painful feelings.

> *Don Juan had taught me to accept my fate in humbleness. The course of a warrior's destiny is unalterable, he once said to me. The challenge is how far he can go within those rigid bounds. If there are obstacles in his path, the warrior strives impeccably to overcome them. If he finds unbearable hardship and pain in his path, he weeps, but all his tears put together could not move the line of his destiny the breadth of one hair. (Castaneda 1991, 110)*

Our destinies are predetermined in certain ways. Our third-dimensional life story and unfoldment is under the control of our higher selves as we come into alignment with it. These higher dimensional aspects of our being only allow the third-dimensional aspect (the human experience) to move within certain predetermined perimeters of this building of life.

Visualize human destiny as a skyscraper with many floors. The length and breadth of the skyscraper represent the limits within which one can move within the boundaries of one's destiny. One is allowed to move freely within the perimeters and heights of the skyscraper. Often people choose to remain on the first floor; some are unaware of the other floors; while others blast through all the potential rooms and floors of the building. Each soul is born with its potential destiny and what s/he is capable of.

Unfortunately, some souls are born in a household where their unique talents (which indicate the soul's destiny) are not appreciated or encouraged. Such souls' potentialities are often pushed in a different direction than what their souls came here to express. There are two distinct kinds of life directions. One is the direction that the soul is born, which is his/her possible destiny. The other is the destiny that is imposed on such a soul after its birth from the parents, social conditioning, television, magazines, movies, etc. To be really fulfilled, one must go in the direction of whatever talents and destiny one is born with. Much of human misery is the result of not following the souls' inspiration or not moving in the direction meant for them. Several healing therapies and meditative practices serve to awaken the soul to its own true nature and to remind the person of their birth purpose.

There are people who believe our lives are determined by our innate nature and tendencies that we are born with, which have to do with personality types. There are also those who argue that the conditioning, programming, values, way of thinking, and life situations that a soul is born into are what determine our life events and path. Both determine our life events. Our lives are affected by the environmental situations and conditioning that we are born into and grow up in, which are programmed by parents, teachers, politicians, priests/pastors, and so on. These are where most of our conditionings and subconscious thoughts (including political, personal, mythological beliefs, etc.) are kept hidden from the conscious mind.

Awakening usually precedes alignment. After experiencing my spiritual awakening, I began to have a sharper clarity about my purpose and life direction.

My third level of awakening occurred while listening to Barry Long's tape one morning. Suddenly, I could feel everything. If I thought of a person, I could feel whatever they were feeling. It felt as if I were feeling the whole planet and like I was processing for the whole of humanity. It was intense and beautiful at the same time. It all just passed through me.

I sensed I could not breathe. I relaxed into it, trusting the process, and as I did so everything went silent. I was being pushed by Grace, and I fell into the abyss of "Ahh"…the eternal now. I was dropping quickly. I knew I was dying, literally, but there was no major resistance because I'd had a death experience before. There was a complete silence combined with a mysterious, loving presence. I died again. I realized that even though I had just experienced "death," the eternal I AM is always Presence, which is what we all are, the part of us that never dies.

It was very much an embodied awakening. It is when the so-called Higher Self, the Soul, anchors into my body. It required my body-mind to be fully transparent, spiritually clear of most of the trauma, and clear of most of the debris. Only then was the Higher Self comfortable enough to descend into my body. From that moment on I realized that everything is being done by the Universe in conjunction with Higher Self and not the egoic mind. With this realization I became aware that life unfolds according to the Divine Will, and that when I live in accordance with the Soul's purpose and a natural sense of alignment with the Universe, my purpose ensues.

Castaneda, Carlos. 1991. *The Eagle's Gift*. New York: Simon & Schuster.

Courtney Ciandella, "What It Means to Trust Your Gut," The Wal flower Blog (blog), December 21, 2021, https://studio-wallflower.com/what-it-means-to-trust-your-gut/.

Oluwa Adams is an iconoclastic mystic, spiritual guide, radical philosopher, tantric depth psychologist, author, singer, and songwriter. His passion is to help people deepen into meditative presence, bringing health, joy, and peace to the body, mind, spirit, and soul. He has a PhD in mythology with an emphasis in depth psychology. As a former professor of philosophy, psychology, and religious studies, he incorporates his skills, knowledge, and tools into teaching meditative presence, tantra, and dance yoga techniques internationally. He teaches freedom through embracing one's inner contradictions and how to integrate them to experience the abundance of love, joy, and peace that resides within each of us. Oluwa is a private coach to those who want to deepen into Presence and heal their heart. He is completing his solo book to help others understand the different dimensions of consciousness, astrology, mysticism, personality types, and global hierarchy. He currently lives and practices in the United Kingdom.

www.facebook.com/olusesan.adamsoyenuga.9
/www.oluwaadams.com/
You can also find Oluwa Adams-Oyenuga on Spotify and iTunes.

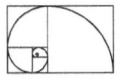

Marina Nash

Lean Into Your Shadows

Our life force smolders deep within us, sometimes buried beneath years of pain. Yet it is always waiting to be excavated and revealed, to reemerge as fresh and wild as broom plants in fields of ash and streams of lava.

In April 2022, my year-long course in Embodied Mindfulness Leadership was coming to a bittersweet close. Day after day of showing up, doing my work, and finding my feet, this marked the beginning of yet another new chapter in my life. What a gift.

It took sixty-two years to arrive here. It's never about the place. It's an arrival at a very intimate connection with self. I finally felt seen, not only by others but by myself. Hearing my self-written obituary read out loud by one of my peers was a raw, gut-bending and empowering experience, something I could never have imagined. I surrendered to who I had been and will become. What was, was. Now is all that matters.

A deep state of acceptance washed over me. I am a seeker. I need to understand. I have always had grit, but this was different. Placing my hands on my heart, I could feel the life force beneath them and acknowledge the tremendous Journey I had been on. It was one with my body, my soul, and my mind; one with nature, my family, my community, and the universe. I felt such an abundance of light and love vibrating through me that it obliterated negative thoughts and feelings. It elevated me to a place where self-compassion trumped true grit. I could begin to open my heart and learn to allow love again.

It has taken a lifetime of crisis, loss, and grief to find my center. A life filled with shards of glass ripping at my core; shattered splinters emanating from family members' mental asylums, prisons, evictions, addictions, and deaths; and the suffocating grip of a pedophile's enmeshed pursuits of me.

Some people learn quickly from experience, while others need to drag out their pain until their soul begs for mercy. I am one of these. I learned to move sideways. Explore the currents. Invite the unknown. Seek the light. Jump in. What finally brought me to my knees was my diagnosis of stage IV cancer, followed three years later by my husband's death from his.

Fear paralyzes. I have lived there. After many years of practice and study, I thought that alignment meant physical balance and posture. It wasn't until my yoga instructor adjusted my pose that I realized how easy it is to fall out physically. It's the focus, intention, and breath work that keeps us steady. Alignment is not perfect, permanent, or static. It's a continuous unfolding into vulnerability. It's failing, falling, then beginning again in order to rise up stronger the next time we seek it.

Pause. Breathe. Hold your heart. Repeat. Alignment doesn't just happen. Being in alignment is a conscious choice. There have been times in my life when I felt aligned: I stood upright, self-confidence circulating throughout my body; I glowed as energy was emitted from every pore of my skin.

And yet these moments were never permanent. It's easy to collapse out of alignment, only to discover another opportunity to arrive at a deeper, more meaningful practice and achieve even greater balance. I've learned that it is the process of practicing throughout a lifetime that brings one closer to that place of inner peace. Nothing is flawless. Smile at your imperfections and surrender to what might be the most beautiful moment of your life.

Sometimes being out of alignment is circumstantial when life is riddled with trauma that is out of our control. That was my norm throughout my life. I didn't know any other way. Survival of the fittest.

Just do it. Then do it again, but better. Climb, run, pedal faster, win at all costs. Although it was familiar and habitual, this was not a state in which to thrive. It wasn't until I could afford my own psychotherapy that I began to understand the deep scarring that had left me numb and incomplete. It had become so embedded that it seemed comfortable. It was my normal.

Warp speed. Everything happening at once, driving me to improve, perform, succeed. Constant crises, obstacles, tragedies. My life unfolded quickly, demanding the agility and attention of a mountain goat caught in a rockslide. Continual bad news became a way of life. Breathing remained shallow. Then, just as I almost regained balance, Wham! Another turn, another twist, another loss.

Find your path, pivot, adjust. Run. Time flies when left unnoticed. Trauma happens with no warning or preparation, leaving unfinished or unresolved relationships in its wake. Moving, switching languages, leaving friends behind for reasons that were not mine, left me shrouded in a dark cloud. The constant changes and shifts were so swift that the only thing that overpowered the excruciating pain of abandonment was shame.

I have finally found the way to my center again. Nature brings me back. She has always been there to capture my eye and warm my heart. She reminds me to breathe. Slow down. Moments filled with wild raspberries and crisp narcissus illuminated my escapes, embellishing my inner landscape and softening the shards of chaos.

Living in the moment can mean different things to different people. In order to survive, one is definitely living moment to moment, hanging on to every breath to avoid being pulled under again; but that is not the same as living in the moment. That is not the kind of presence or awareness that I call alignment.

It has taken me a lifetime to unwrap all the tragedies that affected me, and some still lurk suspiciously in the shadows. If I have learned anything about living mindfully in the present, it is that one must be fully embodied and awake, pause often, slow down to a crawl, and take life in through all of one's senses. Then and only then can one embody the essence of being fully alive.

Grit. True grit. Fall. Get back up and do it all over again. Alignment, if rigid, can be fragile. Allowed to be flexible and resilient, it will be vigorous. Alignment isn't a linear path. It is the process of self-exploration throughout a lifetime of experiences. It flows like a mountain stream emerging at its source, cascading down sheer facades, finally restrained within the lush flora it nourishes. Alignment is the journey where it is natural to get caught in life's distractions, caring for others, getting lost, being found, and searching for inner peace along the way. Sometimes alignment can be accelerated by shock, grief, loss, or trauma, as dramatic and sudden as a lightning bolt searing its way through thickened skins, or a series of compounded tragedies that make their way through the obscure and murky labyrinths of our minds.

I've always wondered why I was born with the gifts of resilience and determination. I am eternally grateful for these attributes. My curiosity, too, is often the source of solutions to my troubles, and I believe that suffering often propels us to seek realignment with our purpose and our values.

My advice is simple to give, though it is difficult to manifest. Surrender. Get back up and face yourself. Do the work. Keep showing up. Ground yourself through your feet and open your heart. Give thanks and love always. This daily practice has become the foundation of my new life. Let it be yours. Alignment reveals purpose. Live well, teach by example, be creative in every way. And lean into your shadow. Darkness always seeks light!

Marina Warren Nash is an artist, designer, and social entrepreneur. Her prolific body of work has been shown worldwide. Earning her master's and bachelor's degrees in architecture and fine arts formed the foundation for her creative career, which includes public art, installations, classical archeology, art instruction, numerous exhibitions, and now writing. She resides in Boulder, Colorado, where she lives and works with her two dogs, Shadow and Peanut. She can be found exploring trails globally and sharing love with friends and family.

www.marinawarrennash.com
TEDx AIMS: youtu.be/I6f2q4wpHyc
linkedin.com/in/marina-nash-b4a013b
m.facebook.com/508167436/
instagram.com/marinanash1?igshid=NmNmNjAwNzg=

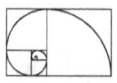

Claudette Anderson

Align With Truth

As if Your Life Depends on It

"Get away from the car!" my dad screamed as I ran outside to greet him. It was his first time home in months. He was working on the car, and it was logical for my three-year-old self to be nowhere near the action. The feeling of being yelled at spiked my entire being with fear and rejection. His greeting was full of anger. I craved his attention, and I know that was too much for him at the moment. His intentions and focus were anywhere but home. I remember him coming back into the house after he completed his work, letting us know that the car would function properly while he was at war.

My mom realized that our brakes failed as we drove toward a highway. We ended up crossing six lanes and landed in a field. As we sat there watching the gas attendants try to figure out the issue, it became evident that our brake lines had been cut. When we returned home, we were informed our bank accounts were drained as well. My father had planned for a devastating accident.

Moving in with my grandparents gave me a sheltered, nomadic lifestyle. Growing up, I was guarded by religion and moved around often. We ultimately landed in government housing. Becoming street-smart and winning a few fights provided me with some amazing friends. This lifestyle was a balance of high-strung fun and immense trauma. I've used these experiences to expand my understanding of this world. If I wasn't strong, I wouldn't survive.

Mom finally remarried a preacher who seemed charming. On the inside he was manipulative, addicted, and relied on sociopathic behavior. I turned inward to block myself from violence. I remember crying myself to sleep at night, thinking of the viciousness my mother was subjected to. I knew I had to protect her, and eventually my brother and I were able to beat him out of the house. Although there was peace once he was gone, a storm began to brew. I was angry at everything I'd been put through, and I focused that energy on myself and my family.

This lifestyle followed me into my first marriage. We were nineteen, I was ready to leave the house and little did I know I would be marrying what I'd previously tried to escape. I told myself, "Either I leave with my suitcase, or he leaves in a body bag." I fought my rage and chose to flee for the safety of everyone. I look back and observe how the anger, stemming from my childhood, was a burning coal to my cancer. I ended up in a new marriage that lasted twenty-three years, which was single-handedly one of the biggest challenges of my life. Every part of me was being tested, and I couldn't feel the love I craved because I had not yet found it fully within myself.

Exhausted and feeling criticized, I contemplated ending my life. I was taking a bath, thinking about the repercussions, and it was as if a presence flashed before me, accompanied with an overwhelming feeling of comfort. Everyone has the ability to perceive this energy; some call it God, or chi, but whatever its name, it is the life force that flows through all. For my own understanding, I call it Truth. There can only be one originating spirit. Once I accepted this, I began to see all the times my life was saved: I had been healed from cancer, and I was always loved. The choice of growth was the only option I granted myself.

A battle raged in me until I discovered that I was the only problem. No one else contributed a single qualm without my acceptance. I previously considered everything an attack against me, and it was time for a less exhausting perspective. By connecting to Truth, I was able to highlight beliefs that I wore like a sash across my heart. Most of these beliefs were fear, doubt, not being worthy or good enough, or having those feelings toward others. Becoming familiar with my beliefs began to shift my internal state into harmony.

Because I worked as a youth pastor for years, I began to question everything I once knew. What do the stories in the Bible actually mean? To me, nothing made sense. So, why do something if it isn't working? When we are sparked to seek further, that is the life principle nudging you out of ego and into the beauty of your individualization. My popularity at church declined as I asked these questions, as it was taboo to question anything. I didn't care. My growth and understanding outweighed the judgment of others. As Truth began to grow stronger in my awareness, I became brave enough to step out of religion and into an authentic relationship with my maker.

The catalyst for the company I proudly call The Truth Method came from someone I reached out to for help. She was an advanced prayer guide. Fear struck me the first session, but it was the beginning of my freedom. *What's scary about that?* Fear is a trick of the ego; it rises in you to stop the creation of what you truly want. It makes you uncomfortable around the idea of learning the Truth. My sessions with her only lasted three months; she didn't think she was qualified to help someone with my level of trauma—trauma ranging from abuse, rape, violence, rejection, and abandonment. I walked out of her office crying, shaking, and feeling utterly hopeless.

"Let's do this My Way." This was the Truth that rose in me as I tried to come to terms with this news. At first my mind was acting like a squirrel searching for a nut. I would get triggered, and my ego would beat me up for not having all the answers. Deep down, I knew I had to keep going for myself, my family, and all who would resonate with this in the future. Just like that, I found myself connecting to Truth without hesitation. This connection gave me solutions to any problem. I began to seek Truth in my business decisions, and in my relationships with my family, friends, and strangers. My overall life began to shift.

The subject of Truth isn't a religious conversation; it is a return to that which you are a part of. It is a journey of individualizing through your life experiences by ridding the negative effects and highlighting the story of growth. Creation is within you and everyone on this planet. Diving deep into the relationship between science and spirituality has been my twenty-eight-year journey with Truth. The presence of Truth dates back roughly thirty thousand years; it is woven throughout cultures.

If you've ever thought there is more to life than meets the eye and that you could be better off than you are now, this is the calling for your perspective of the world to change. We seek answers without knowing where to look. Our misunderstanding lies in the fact we don't know this comes from within us. You may not have experienced all I have, or you may think your life isn't so bad, but regardless, the solutions to the problems that lay before you are already within. I look back and giggle because, in the beginning, I doubted Truth and the ability to shift anything. Now I know without a doubt this is true for all things.

If you begin this journey, it is best to see it through. Why? Your identity, spirit, and the essence of who you are is evolving to a new level of consciousness. You may meditate and feel a difference in the act of meditation, but wouldn't it be glorious to feel that way all the time? With Truth, this is within reach. I didn't start a company, or even share my journey, with anyone else. I did it because I was exhausted and needed to save myself. I was giving up on life; it was too hard. Now, my eyes fill with tears at the beauty of life that stands before me. With Truth, I am brave.

Where there is sadness, it is replaced with joy. The feelings that Truth provides run deeper than any surface feeling. I don't seek approval from anyone but myself and the creative force that constructed me. I was healed from cancer, chronic infections, and sinus issues. I have successfully navigated changes during menopause. And anxiety is so rare that when it happens, the belief that caused it is removed before it has the chance to fuse with my identity. Peace will become your state of being. You can be unshakable.

Check out the links below to start your journey. This practice partners with all spiritual practices and modalities. The Truth cleans up any limiting components. The guidance you receive is like a trusted advisor. *Align with Truth as if your life depends on it, because it does.*

▼ ▼ ▼ ▼ ▼

Awakening architect, facilitator for Truth, entrepreneur, and author, Claudette is ever curious and always seeks to find a deeper meaning. Cervical cancer jolted her into seeking the Truth within herself. She was faced with surgery that would block her health and the ability to grow the daughter she always dreamed of having. Putting her trust in Truth, Claudette began to conceive the beliefs that created the cancer in the first place. This understanding of her subconscious mind allowed her to shift those beliefs and determine why they were allowed to exist. After four months of drastic reflection, Claudette received confirmation from the doctor that she was cancer free. This instance was the catalyst for her twenty-eight-year journey of seeking Truth and helping others do the same.

Through her coaching, online courses, conferences, retreats, and speaking engagements, thousands have stepped into their freedom.

claudetteanderson.com
truthmethod.com
www.facebook.com/groups/truthmethodpublicgroup
www.instagram.com/theclaudetteanderson/

"Your alignment will
be tested after you
meet a goal.
Protect that space
fiercely!"

— Mistilei

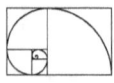

Chaff Amatoury

The People of the Phoenix

Far across the oceans, many worlds away, on a little patch of land
on the other side of the globe,
lies a tiny little country, on the Mediterranean shore.
It's had many names and flags across the millennia.
and you can definitely say it's had its fair share of drama.
Not the richest of countries, nor the most powerful of armies,
No, the wealth of this nation lies deep in its people,
in their strength and resiliency, and their famous capacity
to endure anything and survive, no matter the struggle.
You see those people descend from an old line of resilients.

The Ancient Phoenicians: The People of the Phoenix.

This is where I hail from, and where this journey began. In present day Lebanon, along the Mediterranean shore, I was born during a bloody fifteen-year civil war. You may have seen the news articles or the videos of the nuclear-like bomb that tore through Beirut in August 2020. You see explosions and bombs aren't new for most Lebanese. My mother studied through her whole college education under Israeli bombardment to teach French in the Lebanese public school system, which later funded her law degree. Today she is a judge in the Lebanese Supreme Court. My younger sister did the same and is now also a judge. The women of my family, strong as they are, were not the only ones that paid a heavy price. I have an uncle

I never met. He died in his family's arms trying to save his best friend from bombardment, which he did.

Growing up, my best friend Ceazer and I had big plans to fix that world, to change our stars and save our people, especially from despair. It's funny in hindsight, how ironic life can be.

When a young Phoenician felt the itch for adventure in their heart, he or she would get on a boat and sail far away! They would travel to distant lands and discover new worlds. They would trade and integrate, learn languages and other ways, then return home with a wealth of new culture, goods and ideas. And sometimes, equipped with this new wealth, they would gather new tribes and found cities or communities on a new shore, in a new land.

As a young Lebanese boy, I could not wait to leave home. And since most Lebs are fluent in Frenglishabic (French, English and Arabic), at age twenty, I flew off to study in French-speaking Montreal. Here I was, at the roof of the world, arriving in the worst storm in eighty years, but still feeling warm and fired up inside. I soon found the Quebecers were a people of authenticity and love, friendliness and care. This was a true meeting place of loving souls. I quickly gathered a tribe of kindred spirits and we soon had us a family, a band of good friends who lived, ate and slept together. Needless to say, this excited young man didn't spend much time in class, and next, as you'd expect, fell in love with a girl.

Whereas any American or European can travel to and end up in most countries the very next day, we "Lebs" have to spend months doing paperwork proving we are no danger before we are allowed a visa. So imagine my surprise when said girl offers, through some shady acquaintances, to instantly give me some kind of express citizenship. Young as I was, I fell for it and paid up, and was soon left alone without status or money. I could see now how cold it could get, far, far north on the roof of the world.

The Phoenicians eventually had an empire spanning across the Mediterranean and known world of the time. The way they built that empire, dear friend, was not through conquest or scheming. They invaded no one, and never sought after war. No, The People of the Phoenix were expert seafarers, explorers and builders. They traded with all, and made many friends. They sailed on the waves and seeded the coasts, founding independent communities and city states of freedom.

I am now twenty-six and living in Toronto. No longer downtrodden, no longer a victim. With a loving wife in the states, and a short window until I join her, being the community builder I was, I became a Network Marketer. Funny how challenges often bring out the best of us. I did a lot of growing, and something awoke in me. I found the love of business and helping people get free. There is no better feeling than to liberate people's time and energy for them to truly pursue their passion. Going back home for two weeks to quickly set up US papers, fate shut another door. Ineligible for a VISA. For Life! There I was again, my entire life on hold for a piece of paper. For a traveling bird, there is no worse outcome.

In total, I spent an entire decade married to this angel, eight of which we spent in waiting. Now an experienced fighter, I wasn't going to let this stop us. She waited patiently for me until, after years of hardship, we were finally reunited. But fate, dear Friends, again had other plans. After a decade apart, we were now different people. What a tragicomic chain of events. The cherry on top: with me stuck far away, my entire business in Canada had collapsed.

In the case of the Phoenicians, if they ever made a costly mistake, you could say their generosity led to their downfall. Among their many contributions and trades, they brought purple dye and the Alphabet to the world. They taught the Greeks to read and write, they gave without counting of their wealth, knowledge or ships, which greatly strengthened their eventual enemies. It was only after the Romans destroyed the Carthaginian colony that they rose to their great power, ultimately leading to you, dear friend, reading here, these Roman letters. Should one give without counting, always trying to help? Or should we be selfish, and care only for ourselves?"

After my divorce, I found the perfect investment: a high cash flowing property in downtown Minneapolis which gave me my freedom from my job. I was set once again and back on track to my purpose. The day after I closed, I put in my two-week notice. Exactly one week later, in walks the cutest little redhead with fire in her eyes and many scars on her heart. In true Phoenician fashion, I wanted to help. She was a mother of five and an abuse survivor. I should have caught the Universe's wink at the time, as she literally had angel wings tattooed on her back, but also devil horns hidden beneath her hair. We of course fell madly in love, she with my drive and ambition, and I with her strength despite all her scars. I got her her first property, and helped her quit her job. And together we plunged into real estate investing and started making plans to build our sustainable Earthship and permaculture communities. I thought I had finally found a partner who could run at my pace, someone who could sail alongside me with the same goals of liberating people.

By this time, back home, Ceazer had become a pillar of his community. He owned multiple schools and was a teacher himself. People would pay what they could when they could, and their kids would get an education, regardless. He had an international network of businesses that supported thousands of families. "If one of us makes it, all of us make it!" he always said. He was loved and respected by all without exception. Then I got the news. On his birthday, Ceazer was shot and killed. Why him of all people? Who could wish him harm? I should have been there for him, like my uncle was for his friend. The whole country mourned him. All Beirut was sad. I gave up. I stopped trying. It all felt meaningless now. Why bother? He was the best man I knew. My friend, my Brother, gone once and for all. Not long afterwards, on a cold supermoon night, my redhead ran back to an ex. Right on queue. Figures. Funny how life tends to happen all at once. Sad, how for all the beauty we're blessed with, we can still be so ugly to one another.

The people of the Phoenix today are no more. Their language is dead, their history lost. And all of the cities they built have forgotten them. Maybe in the end, that's the fate of us all.

A peaceful people they were.. They sought fraternity and connection. Wherever their sails were seen, prosperity and community would follow. And if we were to look at their closest descendants, we would see that the Lebanese today aren't that different. From the Americas to Africa, and all over Europe, the common stereotype is "a Leb always lands on their feet." Still ever the world explorers their ancestors were, you will find more Lebs outside of Lebanon than within. Resilient and persistent, they never gave up. And throughout the ages, they always rebuilt.

Here at this stop along my journey, I've learned a lot. I've learned that no matter your age, origin or gender, all people want love, peace, and whether we realize it or not, we all crave community. Hurt people hurt people, but humans, at their core, are GOOD! I also learned that I can bring solutions to people that will liberate them to be with their families. Through Real Estate and other vehicles, one by one, we can give people their power back. Whether through sustainable housing that come with no bills, or passive permaculture that could feed the world, it is within our power to truly change our stars. I've learned that at the end of the day, most of us are running in place, alone. And if we were to just meet each other with intention, then together, we could build a world better than any can imagine!

We came here at a very special time my Friends,

we chose this lifetime intently, with all of its drama,

perhaps we're to clear past generational trauma

we knew it'd be a challenge; if not now, then when?

So should I just forget it, and think only of myself?

Maybe I could give up, and diminish, why care?

Then my work is complete, it would certainly be easy

Is this the Man I'll be, a lonely one-man army?

What would that say to all who came before me?

or the sacrifices of those who brought me to this stage?

You see there's a reason we are likened to this bird,

It's because no matter the scale of destruction or fall,

We always rally, all together, and after the burn,

We always come back, as One, and from the ashes rebuild All!

So No! I will not shrink! I refuse to grow bitter!

I will spread Love and not Fear, I will make this world better!

With an open heart, scars and all, vulnerable and unafraid!

Here stands one last Phoenician, who indomitable remains!

With burning Passion in his Heart, and his friends' voices in his head,

This Fire is my birthright! YOU JUST WATCH ME RISE AGAIN!

because the blood of the Phoenix runs through these veins!

and you cannot kill that which won't remain dead!

From the roof of the world to the shores of the open sea,

I'm here to free my fellow Man, and unleash Humanity!

So, the next time you meet a Phoenician descendant,

ask them of their tale, stop them for a second,

know they came from far, on the other side of the globe,

from a tiny little country, on the Mediterranean shore.

you might just be surprised at the length of their odyssey

but mostly know, dear one, you're sitting with Family.

And to you, dear reader, reading these lines as we part,

thank you for sailing with me, and you can take this as a sign,

from the Universe to your soul, let your inner Flame shine!

And if there's one thing you could write in your story from mine,

May you rise like a Phoenix, my Friend, and never lose Heart!

May you rise like a Phoenix, dear Friend, and forever stay Aligned.

▼ ▼ ▼ ▼

Originally from Lebanon, Chaff Amatoury currently resides in Minneapolis, MN.

He is the founder of Live Asset Properties and Syndication Nation, a collaboration of investors and entrepreneurs facilitating access for everyone into large real estate investments with the principled goal of liberating people's time and allowing them to pursue their dreams and passions in life in the way they see fit.

Passionate about providing people with Freedom and financial literacy, he also teaches Real Estate investing courses with the Minnesota Real Estate Investors' Association (MNREIA)

He is also very active in his community and organizes community building events in the general Twin Cities area such as large barbecues, dance classes, networking events and many others.

His interests include traveling, self-sufficiency, the sciences of achievement and personal and spiritual development.

www.facebook.com/chafff/

http://syndication-nation.com

www.meetup.com/meetup-group-wnfznszc/

"Worry about
yourself."

— Mistilei

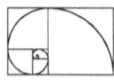

Danielle Olbrantz

Adopting YES LIFE

In 2008 I lost everything. Actually, I lost more than everything, because I was over a million dollars in debt, with quite literally nothing to my name. My car had been impounded, my kids taken from me, I had no place to live, and even my dogs lived with my ex-husband. After an ugly divorce, and with two little kids, I cared more about having fun than I did about all my responsibilities. It started innocently enough, going out on weekends with friends when my three-year-old and eight-month-old were with their dad per our shared custody agreement.

It is amazing how fast it can happen, losing alignment, but for me it was not only fast; it nearly cost me my life. It started as going to a bar on the weekend (something I had never done since I was a mother at twenty-one). My new post-divorce friends were people I respected, a group of other mortgage professionals who all had good-paying jobs, nice cars, and owned homes. We were all in our twenties, and, overall, it was a successful group of people. I was the only parent of the group, but now that I was going through a divorce and had a few nights a week when the kids went to their dad's, I could pretend to be young and kid-less on those days. I lived a double life where I was a responsible mother Monday through Friday, and a single party girl on the weekends. That was something I had never done before. I married my high-school sweetheart, the guy I started dating at fourteen and married at twenty. I had skipped over the carefree twenties, having catapulted directly into adult life with responsibilities.

When I got the opportunity to play the role of a twenty-something without responsibilities, I really thought I *deserved* to experience that.

It worked for a few months. I loved having a social life for the first time, and I was dating one of the guys in the group. One night we went to a local bar, and I had way too much to drink. I was stumbling through the doorway as the group of friends all poured into a small loft-style studio that one of the guys rented. I was not used to drinking that much, and I guess my drunkenness was obvious to others, because one of them pulled me aside and took me to the kitchen counter where they had small lines of white powder. I had never done drugs in my life. In fact, my life to that point had been about trying to do everything right. But that night, inebriation made my decisions. My friend promised me that I would sober up if I did just a tiny line. I honestly didn't even know how to do it, and I was nervous because drugs were never part of my identity. But then again, divorce was never part of my identity either, and here I was with a failed marriage. I decided that all my years of doing the right thing had gotten me to this point, and I deserved to try out the fun things. It seemed innocent enough. After all, these were successful people, and a little partying every now and then couldn't be that bad.

That one tiny line led to a very quick addiction, and for a while I juggled a double life. I kept things together while I had the kids, then I'd let loose when they went to their dad's. But that didn't last long, and soon I was using almost daily and my life spiraled out of control. I had lost all alignment with the real me, and this new identity took over. I won't go into all the details, as that is more than a single chapter, but I managed to lose everything.

I was first introduced to cocaine in July 2007, and by May 2008 my addiction was so bad that I failed to show up for a few days and my ex-husband told me over the phone that he was going to take the kids away. I didn't know how to reverse my spiral, so, in haste, I took one hundred sleeping pills. I really didn't want to die, but what I most wanted was to not be the person I had turned into, and this seemed the way out.

I don't know if I believe in God, but I do believe in The Universe, whatever that means. I know there is a force that is far greater than I am and that, for whatever reason, I woke up alive in a hospital a few days later. It was the wake-up call I needed to make some serious changes.

Alignment, as I define it, is when you are following the plan of the Universe. I believe we all have a defined path that we are meant to follow, and when we leave that path we will likely create massive chaos in our lives. That year, I knew in my heart I was not in alignment with who I was supposed to be. Even as the addiction increased daily, and behaviors that I was not proud of continued, I knew deep down it was not who I was meant to be.

In the years that followed, I managed to rebuild my life, meet an amazing man, get remarried, raise my kids, start businesses, and become overall fairly successful. It took about fifteen years, and it was not easy, but what kept me going was the feeling that I was finally figuring out who I was meant to be. It would have been easy to ignore that feeling, to get wrapped up in the "how" and the "why" and the chaos of life; but I managed to take one step at a time in the right direction without really being able to always explain *why* I was moving in that direction. It was a force that was driving me toward something.

About five years ago, my husband read a book that had to do with saying yes to things. I honestly don't even remember the name of the book, but we started saying yes to things, even things we really did not want to do, like attending a networking event. We would look at each other, shrug our shoulders, and say, "Well, I guess we have to say yes?"

Then things started happening, slowly initially. Saying yes to something would lead to an opportunity, or a new client, or something unexpected. It became almost funny, but amazing things continued to happen. When we started tracking back to when these great things started happening, we realized they tracked directly back to times we had said yes, even when we didn't necessarily want to.

Saying yes became more to us than just agreeing to do things that we didn't want to do. It became our way to get out of our heads and not over-think things. It became our way (before we really even knew it) to create *alignment*. I believe that everyone has the ability to have an extraordinary life and achieve amazing things, but along the way we either stop in our path and choose a different direction, or we fight the Universe and do like I did: totally turn myself upside down fighting against who I was meant to become.

The Universe can present us with incredible opportunities, but we have to be open to following the plan of the Universe. For me, many of my successes and achievements came in unexpected ways. Some of the greatest things in my life happened after what seemed to be horrible events. It was in those times, when things felt horrible, that I allowed myself to accept the situation as it was and continue to take one step at a time in the right direction, being open and willing to trust the process. And in nearly every situation, the final result was better than I could have imagined or planned. The idea of having control over our lives sounds like something we would want, but the Universe often has a better plan than we could ever come up with on our own.

Alignment is that openness and readiness to accept the plan of the Universe. It is when you are moving toward becoming the person you know you're meant to be. It is surrendering to the process, even when it has unexpected bumps. Alignment does not guarantee you an easy road, but it offers you a path to have the most amazing life if you are willing to just say yes without always understanding why.

Danielle Olbrantz lives in Northern California with her husband, Paul. They have four children combined in a Brady Bunch–style family. Danielle is President of Clear2Close, Inc, which is the mortgage processing company that supports Paul's mortgage brokerage, Clear2Close Brokers. They opened their companies in 2019 based on the belief that their customers deserved great rates without sacrificing personal and experienced service. In 2021 they were ranked 49th Mortgage Broker in the United States by Scotsman Guide, and pride themselves on always doing what is right for their clients. Danielle serves all of California and Nevada in their mortgage needs. The couple is also involved in a number of charitable organizations, and for the last five years they have rented a private movie theater each December where they host children from a local group home for a Christmas movie, after which each child leaves with gifts collected from their annual toy drive.

www.myhomeloanteam.com
www.facebook.com/danielleolbrantz
www.facebook.com/myhomeloanteam.com
www.instagram.com/danielleolbrantz
Danielle@MyHomeLoanTeam.com

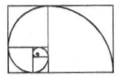

Maryna Grace

In My Time

Here is my secret, a very simple secret:
It is only with the heart that one can see rightly;
what is essential is invisible to the eye.

– Antoine de Saint-Exupéry

Aligning to the true voice of "I" has brought me to extraordinary experiences, romantic love, friendships, business, travel, and, the most delicious of them all, inner peace. If I were to describe what alignment feels like to me, it's like finding that pull point between the plus and minus polarities of the magnet. It's being in the wholeness, both inside and outside, of pleasure and pain, of duality and oneness. It's an experience of 5D in 3D. It's sensorial in the physical and in spirit. To me, alignment feels like knowing. I know, unequivocally, beyond fear, mind chatter, or impossible circumstances. I just know. Truly, I *love* this feeling. It's like tasting God, as if She were the most delicious cupcake.

But—yes, there is always a but—getting to this knowing is not always easy. If you are reading my words and longing to find your way of being aligned to the purest sense of yourself, allow me to share the ways I "plug into this grid" of aligned knowing. Perhaps my ways, my weaving of the tapestry of sensing, feeling, loving, and knowing, will resonate and inspire you.

My invitation to this project came rather last minute. Lovely Mistilei wrote in an email that this is a "right now" project, a sort of Unleash the

Power Within (UPW) of writing. To those unfamiliar, UPW is a four-day event offered by Tony Robbins, a sort of boot camp for your soul. I have attended it three times as part of my Platinum Partnership. Although I'm a devotee of self-development, I skipped the last two UPW events. Quite literally, as my friend brought a pogo stick and we ended up skipping through the hallways in joyful laughter, hugs, and deep talks. There is a reason why I mention it, and why it inspired me to write this chapter: there is no one-size-fits-all process to self-discovery, no single way to become aligned. I loved working with Tony, but many of his techniques and teachings did not work for me. They didn't align with the way my soul craved to be discovered. By discovering what didn't work for me, I found what did, and I gave myself permission to know how I am different.

Being in alignment is different for each human. For some it is a pure, in-the-moment, instinctive knowing. As if life is making a decision through them, as if their internal life force knows exactly what is correct for them, a raw gut feeling. If you resonate with these words, then trust that you are in alignment. For me, however, it's not quite like that. My knowing requires an approach.

I love being in a female body that is capable of experiencing a wide spectrum of sensations and emotions. It is my barometer of alignment. My body loves being loved. When she feels good—in pleasure, in comfort, in beauty, in being attended to—she radiates sunshine, sparkles of bliss, and exudes magnetism. It's as if there is an invisible compass inside my body that clicks into the correct direction, activated by feeling good. The opposite of high-strung, my nervous system is bliss-strung. In this bliss-strung state, my body becomes a cocoon for my intuition, holding it safely, allowing it to sense things freely. This is one piece of the puzzle, or one thread of the woven tapestry in my process of being aligned: *Sensing*.

I move slowly when it comes to knowing something for certain. My "knowing" rarely comes overnight, and I often need to check in with my feelings on a certain question over the period of a few days, weeks, or even a month. As the cycle of the moon takes twenty-eight days to go from dark to bright and full, back to quiet and still, so do my feelings want to flow through each up and down. Only when I have allowed myself the space to feel each side of the wave can I arrive at a pure knowing of what feels in alignment for me. Making a move in the now is not my way. I have tried to bypass this checking-in with my sensing and feeling by just saying yes in the moment, and it turned into a not-aligned nightmare. So now I wait, and I feel through things.

For a big decision, I will give myself a full twenty-eight-day cycle, checking in each day and asking myself, "How does [moving to X place] feel today?" I keep at it until I get a solid knowing in my bones, skin, and soul that it's a yes or no. Until that happens, I wait, and I keep checking in. For smaller decisions, I create an environment where I can step away from being influenced by others' thoughts and energies. I tune into my body through sensing and let my feelings ride the wave of how it feels in expansion and contraction. I am a slow feeler. Those close to me respect this required processing time and no longer push me to decide right away. When aligned in my time, the results have always been miraculous. Allowing myself to know things slowly brings me to the truly exquisite experience of feeling in alignment: *Feeling*.

Did you read *The Little Prince* when you were young? It's one of my favorite books. I remember how it made me feel so understood. It felt like the little prince and I had discovered a secret to life that the adult humans around me could not access. It is only with the heart that one can see clearly. The mind is designed for things like keeping us alive, using correct grammar, not missing our metro stop, or philosophizing on the concepts of good or bad. The heart, on the other hand, is here to bring it all to life. It is the heart that transforms plain words into sweet poetry; it is what turns "eyes meeting" into love at first sight. When attended to, it becomes an internal sunshine that melts away the harshest blocks. It is the vessel of love held within our body: *Heart*.

As a clairvoyant lineage holder, I have always gotten clear reads on people, situations, and places, but it took me years to learn how to overcome the static noise of past traumatic experience and doubt, both of which interfered with trusting in my knowing. I now have many tools in my pocket, each cherished for their ability to keep me aligned to the true voice of "I." This "triangulating knowing" is one of these tools:

- Do I sense...

- Do I feel...

- Does my heart want to...

When all three align, I act. This is my road map to being the creator of my own destiny. This is my quick practical guide to tuning into alignment, of entering wholeness and endless possibilities. When I am aligned in this way, things happen as if out of thin air: A coveted tradeshow gets a last-minute cancellation and offers me a free showcase spot; I meet the love of my life on a "spontaneous" trip across the world I know I have to go on; someone cancels on me, which is disappointing at first but later turns out to be a fraud deal. From big things to small things, living in alignment to the true voice of "I" allows me to experience life and all its possibilities to the fullest. I find all things come to me *in my time.* My wish for you is to create your cycle of sensing, feeling, loving, and knowing—your "I."

What's next for me as I harmonize and align into alchemizing my purpose, passion, and pleasure? I sense, I feel, and my heart wants to step into sharing my knowledge with people, instead of just thriving in alignment within myself. I know that when I am in alignment, I am a force that radiates energetic inspiration into the world. Weaving together my clairvoyant gifts, extensive esoteric knowledge, and sacred travel with my corporate and entrepreneurial backgrounds—along with being sparkled with passion for beauty, aesthetics, and all things pleasurable—I know this is my next step. I know I must walk through the fears of being seen. I know that in this alignment, as I open this door, I will discover a whole new universe. I invite you to follow me into discovery or, until then, join me at the start of each day by aligning to your higher self, the Supreme Being, your angel and spirit guides with a prayer:

Divine Spirit within me,

align me with the direction of my highest good this day.

Align my mind, align my body,

align my emotions, align my words,

so that I am able to be my best,

do my best, serve my best,

and experience the best!

Give them permission to assist you in aligning your day in the most expansive ways. Align to your North Star and claim your miracles.

Aloha

Maryna Grace is a successful entrepreneur, dog mom, and a lady of adventure. She loves knowledge and self-discovery. Her areas of focus are shadow work (Jung), esoteric knowledge (theosophy, philosophy, yoga), somatic embodiment practices to deepen the feminine wisdom of the body, and ancestral knowledge. After almost a decade of being a CEO and "plant witch" of a globally successful, luxury organic skin care brand, Maryna is perfectly aligned to expand her creativity and step further into spirituality and mindfulness. She assists highly evolved souls who have been born into this highly polarized world, helping them align and feel accepted for their unique spiritual gifts. To learn more about your unique gifts or her exciting new product centered around celebrating the inner beauty queen within each woman (and man), please visit her at the links below.

www.mahalo.care
www.instagram.com/mahalo.care

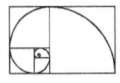

Lis Suppo

Making Dreams Come True

I'm sitting in my backyard on a beautiful Sunday morning mid-September in Greenwich, Connecticut, listening to some chill music while the smoke of the copal I brought from one of my trips from Tulum (Mexico) burns and cleanses my energy. My view of the golf course in front of me never ceases to amaze me.

How did I get this lucky? How did I manifest this life? In my wildest dreams, I somehow knew I was going to have an amazing life, but there's a part of me that still can't believe this is the life I've created.

Growing up in Argentina, I always knew I was born for something bigger and better. I remember a day on my mother's apartment balcony, looking out and thinking, "I have to leave this country one day. I have to move up north." I didn't know where "up north" was. In my mind, possibly the United States, but I really didn't know. I just knew that Argentina was too small for me. The way the people think, the way they act. They are beautiful people and very warm, but I just wanted more from life, more of me.

One day, I found myself thinking, "What if I get to the end of my life and ask what if? What if I had done…or hadn't done…?" I thought, "No, there is no way I am going to waste this lifetime." So when I was twenty-three years old, at the end of my fifth year of university, I decided to leave everything behind to go after my dreams.

The first one was to travel around the world as a backpacker. I'd already intuited that I would have a lot of money in my life. That certainly wasn't the case while traveling as a backpacker by myself in 2002. But I wanted to really get to know people, their culture, and how they lived.

I sold everything I owned. I grabbed a backpack and left Argentina for good.

Making my first dream come true was one of most powerful feelings I've ever experienced. I remember tears falling down my cheeks as I was on the train going into the capital of Italy, the old Rome. I remember being on that train, looking out the window; I embodied the feeling of living my dreams. I knew I had to share this, to help more people know the importance of having their dreams come true. So for almost a year I traveled and stopped in whatever town I liked, found a place to live, got a job, and made a little more money so I could continue traveling.

That was my life, until it came time to make my second dream come true: becoming an actress. I should mention a quality about myself: I always go to the highest possible point and reach for the stars. There is always time and room to go down. I said, "I'm going to New York to become an actress," and in February 2003 I found myself in New York pursuing my second dream.

It wasn't easy. Over the next few years, I found an agent and became a Screen Actors Guild (SAG) actress. Then I met my husband and became pregnant with three kids in one year: twin boys first, then my third boy when the twins were three months old.

My marriage was one of the toughest experiences I have ever encountered, and therein the one where I learned the most. It taught me to get to know myself deeper than I even knew was possible. It took me to places I was not prepared to experience. The darkest nights of my soul were byproducts of my marriage. Even so, the most beautiful thing I learned from my marriage was **unconditional love**. It didn't matter what my husband put me through; I always found love for him. Don't get me wrong, I wasn't an easy wife. I put up a fight, for sure. But then came the point that I thought my soul was dying in that marriage. That's when I was finally able to get divorced.

It was not easy. I was alone in a new country with no family. I had three young kids and no job; however, I had a lot of courage and a lot of will. That's when my spiritual journey really started. That's when I found out that all those years as a child when I thought I was intuitive, it wasn't just intuition. I was a medium.

I went to what I thought was a soul-searching retreat while going through my divorce, but it was a mediumship training instead. It was then I realized how easy it was for me to connect with the spirit world. That is when I found my life purpose, my spiritual path. Finally able to connect with my spiritual guides, I've never felt alone again. It's been eight years since then, and I'm still learning about my gifts and how I want to share them with the world.

After being divorced for five years. my ex-husband and I decided to get back together because we never stopped loving each other. It wasn't a healthy love, but it was better than it was before. We were together for another three years before he passed away in June 2021. During the last six months of his life, it became so clear to me why I had the gift that I had been given, even though it felt worse than any hell I could ever imagine. I knew everything that was happening to me served a purpose. There was always light at the end of the tunnel.

After my husband passed away, I decided to start teaching what I had learned. I decided to help other people *align with whom they came here to be, with their life purpose, and with their higher self, and how to be happy no matter what.* If I could go through hell and come out on the other end, and still become the beautiful being I am today, it was important to share that wisdom with the world, whatever that looked like.

Today my life is aligned with my purpose, my calling, with my very being. I am a spiritual life coach. I get to host retreats in the most beautiful places in the world. I just rented a whole private island in the Virgin

Islands to host a retreat for people who wanted to understand the importance of following their dreams and to know that everything is possible. One by one, I bring beauty and happiness to people's lives because I had a dream as a child and followed my dream. Life is a succession of events. Everything is connected. And I inspire others to find their life purpose. Even when it isn't easy.

▽ ▽ ▽ ▽ ▽

Lis Suppo is a spiritual life coach and medium. Lis coaches one-on-one and creates magic worldwide. She helps people connect with their higher selves so they can live their best lives—the lives they were born to live. She was trained by experts in personal development and spirituality: Tony Robbins, Deepak Chopra, Brian Weiss, and many more. These trainings, together with her natural gift to intuitively communicate with spiritual beings, allows her to channel and guide her clients to become the best versions of themselves, and to be happy no matter what circumstances they are facing in their lives.

www.lissuppo.com
www.instagram.com/suppolis/
www.facebook.com/LisSuppo/

"I hear you.
NOW WHAT?"

— Mistilei

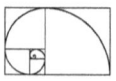

Keith Williams

A Well-Oiled Machine

Alignment could be simple. Like a door hinge or a manhole cover. Or more complicated, like the inner workings of a Swiss-made timepiece or the practiced routine of an Olympic gymnast. When it's right, it's right…it is aligned. It is or it isn't…aligned.

When the alignment is there, the struggle stops. The energy, the effort, is still there, but now struggling does not impede progress. So when I think of alignment, I begin to see the potential for how things should be, how they could be in fact.

It was the late sixties or perhaps the early seventies when I became aware. Aware of myself as an individual. Aware of the world around me. I saw the moon landing on a black-and-white TV, liked The Beatles, and watched *The Partridge Family*. We lived on a ranch with horses and a big red barn. Well, it was big in the eyes of a ten-year-old. I was the youngest of three boys. I thought of my family as close…a team. I felt safe.

The summer of 1970 we planned a road trip that took us from Southern California up the West Coast into Oregon and Washington. At the time we had a two-door, baby blue Volkswagen fastback with a roof rack. And yes, the exhaust had that Volkswagen whistle, and the air-cooled engine burned oil. When we traveled like this it was like a well-oiled machine. Everything had its place. Everything fit just right. When it was finally time to stop driving and camp, everyone had their job. Our tent-camping routine was science, like synchronized swimming.

It was just the four of us: my mother, two brothers, and me. We saw many wonderful things on that trip that I easily recall to this day. While at Crater Lake, a bear came right up to our camp. We went caving, or spelunking (but I did not know there was a word for it). There was an ice cave that prompted us to wear all the clothing we'd brought, as it was summertime. We hiked at Craters of the Moon and went for a dune buggy ride at Oregon Dunes National Park. We stopped in Astoria for a long time, but I did not get the appeal.

One evening we stopped to camp somewhere in the Olympic National Park in Washington state. We pulled up in our spot for the evening and began our ritual of setting up camp. Without a lot of conversation, my brothers, mother, and I took to the task like the team we had become.

There was a couple in the next campsite over that had a legit RV. I could feel them staring at us but could not imagine why. The tent was built, the campfire prepared. The red-and-white plastic table cover was spread out, and the dinner prep had begun when the RV couple came over. They were amazed...floored...aghast at the efficiency of our everyday routine. They asked questions and clearly admired our abilities.

I had no idea it was a big deal because it really wasn't—not to me, anyway. But that couple with the RV made it sound like it was something extraordinary. I felt proud to be a part of this family. Yes, I looked up to my brothers and my mom. We were a team. At that moment, in that campground, with that baby blue VW, my family and I were aligned, a well-oiled machine.

My mom has been gone for several years now. I don't really talk with my brothers much. A lot has happened since that trip up the West Coast. A lifetime of things. That alignment has faded, reappeared, and faded again. I hold dear the memory of that summer a lifetime ago. The process of recollection has warmed my heart.

Alignment can be many things. I am thankful that alignment happened in my life in the Olympic National Forest so many years ago. It can be a simple thing.

▼ ▼ ▼ ▼ ▼

Keith Williams is an accomplished photographer, designer, film maker, and illustrator, and a man of few words. He has been known to stop on the side of the road to look at clouds or to pick up trash, or both. Keith has two grown children and two grandchildren who live in Virginia.

www.keithrwilliams.com
IG @digital.motoart
IG @keithrwilliams
www.facebook.com/krwllms

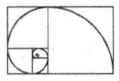

Martha Moon

Bitch

"You *bitch!*" the man yelled when he saw me driving away. I smiled. The term *bitch* literally means a *female dog*. Its original use as a vulgarism carried a meaning suggesting high, *sexual desire* in a woman, comparable to a *dog in heat*.

Whoever came up with that insult never saw a female dog running away from a pack of males trying to mount her. He also had no clue that breeders usually have to tie female dogs for males to impregnate them. And the poor guy sure didn´t have a good sexual connection with women.

Without knowing, I felt rather flattered by the word. The man trying to insult me surely meant it in the definition of the Oxford dictionary:

> *Bitch: (slang, offensive) an offensive way of referring to a woman*
>
> *who you think is unpleasant.*

Hell yes! I was happy to be found unpleasant by that man. I was the *bitch* who stole his *bitch*. Pun intended.

That morning I opened a chat that was put together by animal lovers to save pets lost during the 2017 earthquake in Mexico. Someone posted a photo of a sad pit bull dog chained to a wall in an empty lot. She had no more than four feet of chain so she couldn´t move to get shelter from the sun and rain, nor get away from her own feces. She had no food nor water. And she had an infected wound on her head so deep that you could see the bone.

I didn't even think about it. I just volunteered to go get her, notwithstanding the fact that the lot was in an extremely dangerous area. She was also a *bitch*, not one like me, but used as a bitch. She was pregnant. Abused for breeding and guarding.

In a feminist context, bitch can indicate a strong or *assertive* woman, and Wikipedia includes even more encompassing definitions.[6]

When I approached her, she growled like she was ready to bite my head off if I tried to touch her. How could I blame her? She had experienced nothing but abuse from humans. So I had to bring out the *bitch* in me. "Listen, girl," I said, "I know you are scared but I´m even more scared than you, and we should both be super scared about your owner showing up, so please calm down, I´m here to help." And in a moment of total connection from one *bitch* to another, she stopped growling and turned her head the other way to let us cut through her collar. She even helped us dig under the fence, and when she made it outside she ran like her life depended on it, like claiming her freedom for the first time. I thought we had lost her but to my surprise she made it to the corner and sprinted back to us and got in the kennel with no hesitation. She knew exactly where to go. She knew what was happening. She knew she was safe, and her mission was just unfolding.

Animals have a connection with the source that has always fascinated me. They are always aligned with their habitat, with nature, with others. They live in the present moment while using all the knowledge from their experiences. This is something we as humans cannot experience easily. We have spent centuries making up religions, coming up with philosophies, searching for spiritual practices. All of it as an attempt to find some alignment with ourselves and the universe. And most of us still have not achieved it. Maybe from time to time, during a good day of meditation, or a fortunate yoga practice that made us feel connected for a marvelous but fleeting moment. Or through a plant medicine ceremony that showed us a flash of what being aligned feels like but faded away a few days later if we were lucky.

But for animals it's no effort. They don't need to spend their lives searching for that presence and connection. They don't have to pursue alignment. They are born with what we, humans, have longed for throughout our entire existence on this earth.

There are several studies about how the cattle, deer and some wolves always stand in the same position in relation to the cardinal points. Schools of fish and flocks of birds move in a highly organized way. Individuals adapt their orientation and speed to that of their neighbors. Adaptation of orientation can also be found on the cellular and sub-cellular level and is called alignment:

> *Alignment is a spontaneous behavioral preference of particular body orientation that may be seen in various vertebrate or invertebrate taxa. Animals often optimize their positions according to diverse directional environmental factors such as wind, stream, slope, sun radiation, etc. Magnetic alignment represents the simplest directional response to the geomagnetic field and a growing body of evidence of animals aligning their body positions according to geomagnetic lines whether at rest or during feedings is accumulating.*[8]

So, if animals naturally have the connection to the source and planetary energy that we are so desperately looking for, why do we insist on looking for answers everywhere but there? We need to see the loyal beings that we have always had right in front of us, next to us, if only we hadn't decided to look down on them, and use and abuse them as expandable resources for food, unnecessary cruel testing, clothing and commodities?

The Indian sacred text Bhagavad Gita states that there is a moment in the spiritual path that we must realize that our true teachers are not to be found as humans but in the connection with nature. Are the animals and trees our real spiritual teachers? Have we perhaps always been in the presence of the beings that we should imitate and learn from, and we have been so egocentric, greedy and blind that we have not even noticed?

If you ask this *bitch*, I'd say YES.

I have been blessed with having been rescued by a dog, Leia. A stray *female dog* who has become my teacher, my family, my guide. She has taught me unconditional love. Presence. Gratitude. Resilience. Strength and *courage*. She has taught me how to be a *bitch*. How to be *assertive* and act for what I believe in.

She inspired me to rescue hundreds like her. And one by one I got more convinced that they are indeed our spiritual teachers. Beings full of love and connection, who still turn the other cheek when abused by a human. The story of each one of these beings would make any human ashamed. And inspired.

And that is my mission. Showing the world that we have what we've been longing for right next to us, right under our nose. There are over twenty-five million homeless animals in Mexico alone. Hungry, cold and sick. And willing to transform the life of a human if given the chance.

That pit bull *bitch* who was kept chained as a slave saved the life of the little girl in her foster home. She was able to notice a gas leak that was slowly killing her as she had been sick for weeks and no one knew why. The leak was subtle enough to pass unnoticed by humans, but not to her. Later she got adopted and has since helped dozens of abused women as a therapy dog in a women shelter. Women that were often called *bitches* by their abusers learned the empowering side of the word through that pit bull's story and emotional support.

I am blessed for having witnessed hundreds of stories like hers. Amazing stories of rescue dogs that rescued humans.

"Why do you rescue animals while there are so many children suffering in the world? Do you love animals more than people?" I get asked often. Not at all. I *admire* and *respect* animals more than I do most people I know, I won´t deny that. But it is precisely my love for humans that has driven my dedication to creating Dog Heart Foundation. Because I believe that animals save us, heal us, help us align. The mission of the foundation is to rescue and heal stray and abused animals in Mexico, train them as emotional support or assistance dogs and rehome them to people around the world that need them and could not otherwise afford them. Therefore, finding loving homes for them where they can be valued, and where they can fulfill their mission to rescue a human back into alignment is inestimable.

I am so grateful for the alignment that brought so many *bitches* into my life. *Bitches* barking, *bitches* healing others, *bitches* publishing books, *bitches* empowering other *bitches*…helping each other align.

[8]https://www.sciencedirect.com/science/article/abs/pii/S1616504712000754

Martha Moon Gutiérrez was born in Mexico and has lived in many countries. She holds a master's degree in social sciences and is working on a master's in animal assisted therapy. Producing a documentary for human rights and environmental movements and her own passion to relieve suffering started her on a spiritual path to heal herself and others. A musician, holistic therapist and certified Jivamukti and Hatha Kaula, Yoga instructor, she developed a method of Neuro-Yoga in which she combines Dzogchen Buddhism, therapeutic Yoga; holds the lineage of Kaula Tantra, a method to relieve emotional suffering; and uses neuroscience, psychiatric nutrition and bio-decodification in her work. In 2017, her spiritual practice shifted to the rescue, rehabilitation, and rehoming of stray and abused animals from Mexico. Her current focus is on Dog Heart Foundation, her new project which combines her love to help both animals and humans by training rescued emotional support and therapy dogs for people who need them but can't afford them.

moonmarty@me.com
www.facebook.com/marthamoonneuroyoga
www.dogheartfoundation.org
www.facebook.com/adoptalovemx/
IG@adopta.love

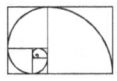

Phyllis Goughnour

Aligning Head to Heart

When we align our head to our heart, *shift happens*. Each of us has the power to direct and create this shift and discover who we really are. We do this by applying three steps: acknowledge, allow, and align.

When I speak of the heart, of course I am not talking about the literal blood-pumping organ, but the heart that is an amazing energy center. I have discovered ways to clear out the clutter that separates our head from our heart, how to align our head to our heart, and to become all we are destined or fated to be. We do this by focusing on our thoughts, words, and emotions.

Let us start by acknowledging that we cannot fully comprehend a notion or idea until we can feel it with our hearts. Which is precisely why feeling an experience is the best way to learn. We remember ideas and thoughts better when we associate them with feelings, which are often triggered by one of the senses, such as a familiar smell, sound, or lyrics.

When I did a deep dive into my thoughts and emotions, it was the beginning of remembering who I really am. I began sorting through the illusions of my life, the journey that seemed so predictable, the thoughts and emotions that kept me doing and feeling the same things over and over. Where did these thoughts come from? Were they even my thoughts? It seemed many of these thoughts were on an infinite loop. It also appeared that the sad thoughts were repeated with greater frequency than the happy thoughts. How did these thoughts affect my feelings? Were these thoughts creating my emotions on a subconscious level? My answer was a definite *yes*, followed by a quick question: How did they affect my reality? It was an easy conclusion that in order to have the life I wanted, I needed to regulate my thoughts before they subconsciously created emotions that I may not desire.

Upon reflection, I realized I was allowing unconscious thoughts and emotions to create the illusion of my reality. On a subconscious level, I was an *inactive* participant in my own reality. I was letting my thoughts and emotions interact without me actively observing and monitoring them.

Which led me to an important distinction: to actually direct my thoughts and feelings, I must first quiet my mind. Once I really quiet my mind, I have the opportunity to understand that I am so much more than my thoughts, emotions, and physical body.

Anyone can do this, and, yes, it requires discipline. By learning to quiet your mind, you discover who you truly are: a divine soul living in a human being form. Everything—every thought, every emotion you have ever experienced—is subjective, offering an infinite number of perspectives. You may even begin to realize that you are a multidimensional being having multidimensional experiences; however, this concept will indeed take another chapter to explore.

How to begin? Spend time in the quiet without the intrusion of subjective thoughts so that you may understand or begin to understand who and what you truly are. Everything you are searching for can be found by going within yourself. You may understand a concept in your head, but you cannot actually own it until it lies in your heart. This happens through experience. To experience means that you understand how it feels. There is no better way to learn something than by associating feelings to an idea or thought that is based on our prior experiences or belief system that was programmed previously.

What does this really mean? It means facing what you have created in your mind. It means being accountable for what you have created and not blaming others or playing a victim or martyr role. You have to monitor those thoughts that are playing on a loop. You are the master of your own experience. Only you can do the work of removing every undesirable thought. Your mind has been preprogrammed to keep playing negativity on a loop. These thoughts need to be replaced or removed before they become an automatic, adverse feeling.

This takes patience and practice. You can only master your universe by consciously, deliberately creating it. This begins by controlling your thoughts. I started by simply recognizing and identifying the thoughts that were not consciously mine, those that just kept repeating from memories or past experiences. When such a memory or thought would pop into my consciousness, I would repeat Ho'oponopono. This is an ancient Hawaiian prayer I learned in Maui. It is made up of four powerful phrases: *I am sorry. Please forgive me. Thank you. I love you.* I would repeat this five times in a row and really feel the words as I said them out loud. This would make my heart happy, and it also "pushed" the undesirable thoughts right out of my consciousness.

Many people think of the Ho'oponopono as the forgiveness prayer. Forgiveness is important, but there is so much involved, such as repentance and transmutation. It is about healing and releasing any negativity to create freedom. In my case it opened up space occupied by the negative thoughts and made space for more desirable or positive thoughts. For example, when someone would cut me off in traffic, I habitually reacted in a not very ladylike manner. To change this habit, I now say out loud, "Cancel! Disconnect that thought." Then I replace it with Ho'oponopono. If I am in the car by myself, I will say it out loud. It enables healing and releasing negative thoughts. I like to think of it as *alchemizing the negative into the positive*. To keep with the traffic analogy, my process (which I hope will help you alchemize negative feelings) is when I hit an extra red light or when I am delayed and getting frustrated, I say "Thank you!" I show this gratitude to the universe because I know in my heart that I am avoiding an accident or I am being directed to the path I need to be on.

When we live our lives with an open heart, we can trust that we will not be led astray.

Much of our conscious lives are dominated by remembering the past or worrying about a future event. These are wasted thoughts! We need to be in the present, now moment. The past is gone, and the future is what it will be. In order to counteract this habitual behavior, when I find myself concerned about what has or what may or may not occur, I redirect my thoughts by focusing intently on the present moment. I look at the clouds or the trees and find such joy in their beauty. I observe the people around me and wonder, "Do they know how divine they are?" By keeping my mind focused on the here and now, I eliminate the possibility of worrying about a future event.

Visualization is another technique I use when I am aware that an undesirable thought has popped into my head. I picture the thought turning into cartoon hearts and exploding. Sounds simple, but I have to begin by letting go of the negativity. If the thought(s) are persistent, I let them rise like bubbles, then turn into hearts. This is something I repeat as needed. Gaining control of thoughts is always a work in progress.

The next step is to allow. This is done by feeling the emotion. Feel it right now! Put yourself, in your mind's eye, into a fun, enjoyable situation. You need to really feel the joy, peace, or love that you want to create in your life. Put a smile on your face and breathe in joy.

Now we need to align our head to our heart. I like to start aligning by breathing in and out of my heart while I am smiling. I feel the love that my heart wants to "breathe" in and out. Along with the smile on my face, I picture a big smile on my heart as it is breathing the joyful feeling in, then out. Sometimes I picture myself as a Care Bear, with my animated heart beating outside my chest, sending love out to the universe, and I realize that when life throws me heartache and I close up my heart, I will not get to the healing that an open heart can teach me.

Let's revisit our three steps: acknowledge, allow, and align. Think of it this way to remind yourself to align your head to your heart. First, acknowledge that the thought is there. Allow yourself to transmute the thought, then alchemize it into the feeling that will align with your heart.

I used the "acknowledge, allow, and align" method to create my marriage. In January of 1998, I decided that I was ready for a life partner and relationship. I acknowledged this by writing myself a letter and being very specific about what I wanted. I included beaucoup details, such as personality traits and characteristics of my future mate. I then added details to the ring and the honeymoon I wanted. Knowing the universe is generous, I tested it a bit and asked for a four-carat diamond and a trip to Bora Bora. I threw in a 20 percent increase in pay and a new Lexus as well. After I wrote my detailed letter, I sealed it and put in in my nightstand and allowed the universe to deliver. I aligned my head to my heart and only allowed feelings of gratitude—as if it had happened in past tense. If a doubtful thought popped into my head, I replaced it by saying, "Thank you for delivering even more than I wrote!"

Ten months later I met my future husband, and everything fell into place, just as I had written it. My diamond was only three and a half carats, but we did go to Bora Bora on our honeymoon. I received and accepted a job offer that was well over the 20 percent I had originally requested. My good friend asked to buy my current Lexus, and we went together to pick out my brand-new one.

I hope my example will help you to align with the infinite being that you truly are, to recognize your limitless potential, and to create abundance on all levels: energetic, emotional, physical, and financial. When you take control of your thoughts and emotions, you become a powerful creator. May this story help you create your own personal power to align your head to your heart so your shift can happen. You can align everything you want in your life when you become the master of your thoughts and emotions.

Phyllis Goughnour is an accomplished business professional with experience in consulting, telecommunications, and the finance industry. She left her engineering degree behind to pursue a rewarding life in service to others. A founding board member of a community bank, Phyllis is known as an innovative thinker who is always looking for ways to improve the world around her. Her spiritual path started when she was a teenager, then she attended A Course in Miracles, which ignited a passion in her to help others find their own spiritual paths. This passion led her to become a teacher and coach, healer, and mentor, helping people remember who they truly are so they can create the life they desire. She feels most fulfilled when she can make a difference in someone's life. Her work is based on understanding that we are all powerful creators who have the ability to manifest our deepest desires, even when life offers challenges and struggles. She helps others *innerstand* that God is in everything and that each of us is God.

www.facebook.com/phyllis.goughnour
www.LinkedIn.com/in/phyllis-goughnour-a38bb11
www.wealthgrowthfund.com

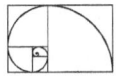

Pierre Elmaleh

Self-Love

I came out to my parents at the age of forty-two.

These few words symbolize my self-inflicted punishment, my sentence for many years. It is as if I were talking about someone else, a stranger whose life in the "closet" must have been miserable. Oddly enough, that wasn't the case at all.

I am Pierre Elmaleh, a French Jew from Paris whose parents emigrated from Morocco when I was four years old. I had a beautiful childhood with a loving family but from an early age I felt different. I was attracted to men, not women.

This realization tortured me. How not to disappoint my parents? How to hide the truth? If they knew it would kill them or the shame would destroy them. For decades that was my belief, so I lived a double life. I had girlfriends, broke a few hearts and fled three times before being engaged.

In my twenties, my needs for *adventure* and *growth* led me to travel the world. I climbed Mount Everest, crossed the Sahara, sailed the Galápagos and dived off Borneo. Spiritually, they led me to travel within myself. This chapter is about the intimate journey to align my body, my spirit and my soul.

It sounds simple: *happiness is the alignment between your brain and your heart, the coherence of your thoughts, feelings and actions.* You may ask, How is this done? My answer: Don't get into your head; let your intuition guide you. Trade fears for faith and allow the universe to bring everything you need, probably in the most surprising ways!

Let's start my story at a different beginning. I met John, my first boyfriend, at the age of twenty-nine. I had no idea we would live together for twelve years. The first time I visited John I noticed a crib in his studio.

"Do you have a child?" I asked.

"Yes, my son Leo is two years old. He stays with his mom half the week and we co-parent. She is a lesbian. We met through a classified she placed in a gay magazine."

John and I raised Leo together for twelve years, from the age of two to fourteen. Leo is my stepson, and we have a beautiful bond. *Growth* is my engine, my most important need and my driving force. When I realized we were not growing as a couple, I decided to leave. My intuition was to start over and I chose to put an ocean between us by moving to the United States.

My new boyfriend in Miami gave me an ultimatum. He said, "No way am I going to return to the closet twenty years after coming out!" So there I was, gathering all my courage as I faced my parents. "Someone is going to live with me, but it is not a woman. It is a man; he is my boyfriend."

Reaction of my mom: "So, you are gay? Is it permanent?"

Reaction of my dad: "So, it means you will not have any children!"

I convinced myself I was doomed and defective. Numerous events seemed to confirm this. I was miserable as a management consultant and quit to become an entrepreneur. I tried an IPO for my mobile phone company exactly when the dot-com bubble burst. I had an eyewear distribution company and my main supplier went bankrupt. I got into the real estate market just before it crashed in 2008.

I told myself, "Certainly, being gay is jinxing everything; it is the reason why I am unlucky."

I needed to make a shift and RE-mind myself of my true worth. The wake-up call came with the passing of my father. His words haunted me. He waited for me to fly to Paris to be present for his last breath. I decided I would be a father too. One life leaves, another would arrive! And so began my journey into surrogacy.

I learned the hard way that co-parenting with a lesbian was not an option. What would I do if the mother of my child fell in love with an Australian? Move to Australia?

The universe took me to an agency in Moscow. The day I signed my surrogacy contract, my life changed. I had purpose. My feelings and my brain acted in coherence. My wings began to grow. I shifted from doomed to lucky, from broke to rich. Real estate became easy and fun. The world smiled at me. I purchased a villa on the water, called "Villa Marina" after the name of the previous owner, a Russian Jew.

My best friend introduced me to the Landmark Education. I learned that self-development meant reweaving the thread between my calling and my actions. I needed to align them by listening to my heart, by being laser focused on my *why* while hushing the *how*.

Self-love is the key to open all doors.

So how does it play out in these moments of decision that shape our destiny? Let's look at a few. They are so vivid given the deep emotions associated with them.

1. I am in Kyiv having an ultrasound done of my baby. It is a girl, she is going to be a Pisces, a water sign and is Jewish and Russian. Of course, her name will be Marina. During the war in Ukraine, the US embassy refused to issue a visa to my seven months' pregnant surrogate. What to do? I take her to Paris where we pretend to be a couple as surrogacy in France is a crime and I could go to jail.

2. My stepson is a physician and puts me in contact with an obstetrician friend. He practices in two maternities in Paris, including Clinique Nicolo. Synchronicity again! This is the same maternity where my mom gave birth to my younger sister forty years earlier. I knew the name because when we were kids, I would make my sister believe she had been found

in a dumpster on rue Nicolo. What a twist of fate to learn my daughter would be born there!

3. Dilemma: If the mother is on the birth certificate, she has parental rights. If she is not, my child could be kept by social services and offered for adoption by "normal couples."

4. At the US Embassy, I am asked, "Where is the mom? We cannot give your daughter a visa without the mother who is on the birth certificate! Are you kidnapping this child?"

During each of these moments, I felt an incredible strength. I was unstoppable because my purpose as a dad was stronger than any obstacle. As I waited over one hour at the embassy, I pondered all possible scenarios. If I didn't obtain a visa, I would need to sell everything and start all over again in Paris. But I had faith. I knew Villa Marina was expecting its little wonder.

I asked abruptly, "Do you realize the power you have over my life? You literally can destroy all I have built! Do you have kids yourself?" These words, coming from a place of truth and vulnerability broadcast intense energy. Deep emotion boosted my eloquence. The officer paused, stared at me and granted my petition.

A couple of years later, I met my now ex-husband. We chatted nonstop about family, our sisters and our moms. His little niece was the same age as my daughter. Perfect! We clicked, we got married and began raising Marina together. This might have been a fairy tale, but we were not aligned.

In retrospect, I realized I probably got married because it had a taste of the lost paradise of my previous relationship. I was reproducing the same love triangle pattern. However, it was not his blueprint, it was mine. For him, being a stepdad filled his need for significance, but gradually his insecurities blew everything apart.

"I am the third wheel," he would say. His demands, his anger, the constant negativity and drama destroyed our lives, my business and my health. I told him it was OK, that we were a love triangle and that every angle has the same worth yet I ended up in the emergency room. My heart was sick, physically and emotionally. The stress of being with the wrong partner was killing me!

"*I resist so I exist*" was my husband's way of being. It rhymes, but *Ego and Love* will never rhyme and I began to dread coming home. I needed to act to repair our relationship—so I dragged him to a couple of Tony Robbins seminars. For me, *growth* is necessary; for him, the uncertainty of growth and uncharted territory are scary. "You want me to come to this seminar because you believe there is something wrong with me," he would argue, "you are trying to fix me." Finally, I came to the realization that he was resenting my being Marina's genetic father. I simply could not win.

When we got married, I believed we had the base to build a beautiful relationship. All I cared about was that he would love my daughter. That was my mistake. I had forgotten myself in the equation. One needs to love and feel loved. I was misaligned.

The pandemic pause and self-development work enabled my transition and my rebirth. I learned how to manifest and become the magnet of my dream life. One exercise I used was to identify a moment of past happiness and extrapolate new possibilities—my intuited future.

Dream 1: Horses

As a teen, I was an equestrian. In my twenties, I did a horseback riding safari in Tanzania, galloped amongst zebras and giraffes with Mount Kilimanjaro as a backdrop. I felt intense happiness and love for the magic of life. My intuition was that if I were to allow horses back into my life, the energy created would foster the happiness I wanted. One month later, I secured a ranch and two horses for me and my daughter. My husband's resistance and jealousy were exacerbated. His negative energy shattered our lives and my daughter paid the price. He made a scene, we were angry, she broke her tibia in the paddock (a metaphor of our broken relation-ship) and I divorced him.

Dream 2: Gay-dads.org

The need for contribution is key to fulfillment. I visualize my partner and I hosting an annual gala for our nonprofit to help finance the dream of surrogacy for future gay dads. It is the calling I am manifesting today. So, stay tuned!

Remember:
Self-love is our intimate diapason.
Its unique vibration broadcasts our soul's energy
and attracts our dream life.
It is magical.
Try it!

Born in France into a conservative Sephardic Jewish family, Pierre had a beautiful and privileged childhood in Paris. He earned an MBA, practiced as a management consultant with Accenture, an entrepreneur, a real estate broker, a general contractor and a globe-trotter who learned ten languages. It looked like all the fairies had cast their best wishes on him. Except he is gay! Because being a dad was his calling, being gay was not in his plans. Between Paris and Miami Beach, where he now resides, Pierre took leaps of faith to find himself. Learning from his mentors, Tony Robbins and Joe Dispenza, Pierre had the courage to follow his intuition and his heart. Now aligned, he acknowledges the power of self-love and gratitude. Proud father of an eight-year-old equestrian daughter through surrogacy and a thirty-one-year-old plastic surgeon stepson, Pierre knows his story proves everything is possible. When aligned, everyone can become anything one sets his mind to. His mission today is to help prospective gay dads have their dreams come true and for his own dreams to flourish.

www.gay-dads.org

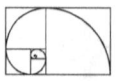

Ruth Hiller

The Accidental Businesswoman

"This is my story about my brand and my journey to design a new life."
I call myself the accidental businesswoman. I've faced a lot of fears and
taken risks, and had the courage to act despite my fears.

Let's talk about fear and how most of us want to avoid feeling fear.
What are we afraid of? There are many fears to consider:

Fear of the unknown

Fear of losing

Fear of dying

Fear of change

The question is, What fear is holding you back? For me it was a fear
of business and spreadsheets. I studied art in school. I didn't have a clue
about business. Partly it was because, as an only child raised by an angry
mom and an emotionally unavailable dad, I didn't grow up with confidence or a belief in myself. My mom always asked me, "What the fuck is
wrong with you?" Not having an immediate answer, I stayed silent. I was
a shy, scared child who felt like I never fit in.

Having always loved art and design, I decided to pursue it as a career,
even though (or perhaps because) my parents disapproved. My parents
always said, "Study something you can make money at." I ended up with a
design degree and a job in NYC. This might seem like a big deal, but after
seven years I felt unfulfilled. I wasn't making a difference in the world. I
was lost and depressed. I bounced around, trying different careers as a
designer, personal trainer, and fine art painter. In 2017 I hit rock bottom

and had no idea what to do. It was there, on the bottom of the rock, I started to look at the patterns of my life. I unearthed the notion that it was time to make a change.

That was the beginning of a five-year journey. I decided to take a break from art to find out what I really wanted. I feared the unknown and didn't know where I was headed. In December 2017, based on a recommendation from a friend, I ended up at a Tony Robbins event that changed the course of my life and my identity.

I knew nothing about Tony and thought he was some weird business guru. When Tony said, "Welcome home," I knew *I fit in*. This was the first time I'd ever felt this. Within the first fifteen minutes of the seminar, I felt like I'd been struck by lightning and had become a different person. I had been medicated and depressed for over fifty years, and I knew in that moment I would never do or be either ever again—and I haven't.

I was blown away by Tony and his teachings. For me, he was a practical psychologist and a miracle worker, providing the impetus to transform my whole identity and step into a new life. My friends didn't recognize me when I came home. After I returned, I went to thank my friend for sending me there, and she said, "It's so weird. I've never done any of his work and am not sure why I sent you there but am glad I did!" Clearly, this was not a coincidence!

Tony's work gave me all new tools to navigate the life I was creating. The biggest lesson I learned from Tony was how to add value and help others. The accidental businesswoman was born. I had always bought and sold real estate but never considered it a business.

Fact: I come from three generations of multifamily apartment owners. History: in 1940, my grandma's husband died and left her with three kids. She traveled to LA and bought three multifamily buildings. She only had an eighth-grade education. How did she know to do that? These properties supported her and her family until the day she died at ninety-six! My parents also bought multifamily apartments in 1968, so I always saw the power of real estate and apartment ownership.

Do you believe in fate? On a bus in Malaysia, I sat next to Brad, who would change my life. When I asked him what he did, he told me that he taught people how to invest in and buy large multifamily (MF) properties. Weird. I told him, "I own one. I need help. Could you help me?"

I was a 50 percent owner with family members, and let's just say the partnership wasn't great. Honestly, in the beginning I really wasn't interested in the business, I just cashed the check.

I did not know a thing about running a multifamily business. Spreadsheets scared the shit out of me. My partners treated me poorly, and this is where I learned to stand up for myself. I was ready to quit and wanted to give up trying to work with them. They were worthy opponents and my biggest teachers.

I wanted to learn, so I joined Brad's program and dove into learning all I could about MF. He inspired me and believed in me before I believed in myself. Was it a coincidence that I met him that day? I don't believe in coincidences. I believe in lessons that put us in alignment with our purpose.

Did you know that 90 percent of commercial real estate is operated by men? I am a woman in the male-dominated field of commercial real estate. When I talked to women friends, most hadn't heard about multifamily complexes or didn't know they could own part of one. I also met many women who didn't have a clue about investing other than in the stock market. I had my first inkling about becoming a woman helping women invest in multifamily properties.

OMG, the spreadsheets! Yet I dove deep into learning the ins and outs of running a multifamily business. The opportunities excited me. I told everyone I knew what I was doing. Friends saw my excitement and wanted to know more, telling me, "We'll have what you're having."

With Brad's encouragement, I joined his mastermind and decided to go all in. I placed myself in a highly successful group of people and felt like an imposter at the first meeting. But I stuck it out! It was through the uplifting environment at that mastermind that I learned about my super-powers in business: influence, connection, teaching, and communication. I decided to start a company to help educate women on how to passively invest in real estate. Brad told me that if I didn't use my name, my business name had to be bold and memorable. I called myself The Accidental Businesswoman but didn't feel the name would generate confidence with investors. So, what would I call it? What best represented my new identity?

- I had to be clear about who my audience is.

- I wanted to create impact and help others.

- I wanted to use my creativity.

- How would I bring value to this new world?

- How would I combine my newfound business sense with my creative side?

- Who would be interested? Would anyone care?

I wanted something that conveyed fun and excitement amid a sea of blue in the financial business world. If the name isn't a "hell yes," then it's a "hell no." Sitting in a branding session, I was brainstorming and YESMF came to me. I don't know what you are thinking, but MF stands for multi-family! It was perfect. It is funny. It is bold. It's fabulous. It fits my personality. I love the double meaning!

Should you invest in multifamily? Yes, motherfucker, you should! I love MF! It's the most widely used curse word in the English language. Motherfucker can be a compliment or an insult.

- You stupid motherfucker: insult

- You badass motherfucker: compliment.

- Let's go, motherfucker: either way.

OK, so now what? I had a cool name and brand, but how would I start a new company at age fifty-nine? What was I thinking? Was I up to the task? What if I failed? Even though I'd earned adequate money at my careers, I never felt financially successful. I wanted to prove to myself that I could create exponential wealth in this business. And I felt incredibly aligned about making a difference for women.

It was time to act and learn how to run a business. It was scary. I was way outside my comfort zone on so many levels. I knew, though, that being outside of the comfort zone is where the magic happens. Remember me saying I never felt like I fit in? Well, now *I don't fit in because I stand out!* I learned I had to create change and inspire myself before I could even think of inspiring others. I had no idea that following a small idea would turn into such a large passion. Design and creativity are not just for art and architecture. I've learned how to navigate using these in the world of business. I found out all the resources in the world didn't get me where I wanted to go. I had to become resourceful. I've come full circle as a creative person in the business world. My business meets my needs in two ways:

1. I get to improve the communities for our tenants in the properties we buy
2. I get to help women take charge of their financial freedom and create wealth

These were the signs I was looking for. I am home. I'm proud of the woman I have become over the last five years.

YESMF, it took perseverance.

YESMF, it was fun.

YESMF, it wasn't easy.

YESMF, I didn't quit

YESMF, I get to make a difference for myself and others.

YESMF, I'm so glad I took the chance on myself.

You can too! Say YESMF. It all starts with a belief in yourself and a step to take action.

Ruth Hiller, from Boulder, Colorado, is a multifamily investor and syndicator at YESMF. Ruth is currently a limited and general partner in over fifteen multifamily deals totaling 2,800 apartment units across six states. She comes from three generations of multifamily owners and furthered her education by joining a multifamily mentoring group. Her BFA in design and packaging have given her a foundation for creativity in the business world. After pivoting from a successful art career into multifamily real estate, Ruth is passionate about helping women grow wealth and passive income through multifamily investing. She provides education and teaches due diligence to help women feel empowered to start investing. When not working on the business, Ruth can be found enjoying nature and traveling with friends. "Success Leaves Clues" - Tony Robbins

yesmfnow.com
www.instagram.com/yesmfnow/
www.linkedin.com/in/ruth-hiller-5517671/
www.linkedin.com/company/yesmf/
www.facebook.com/yesmfnow

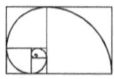

Rhonda Alderman

Your Inspiring Light

I write today with love and compassion for you, whoever you are and wherever you are in life. Reflecting on the many inward and outward journeys I have taken has revealed times when I've lived in alignment, and others when I was not in alignment. My intention is to share in such a way that my story may inspire you, to persevere no matter what and find your own inner light and divine purpose in life.

I struggled as a child searching for love, security, and acceptance from my father who was abusive physically and emotionally. When I was eleven years old, my dad was diagnosed with a brain tumor in conjunction with acute alcoholism. As a result, he had a brain surgery to have the tumor removed, which he survived, but something caused him to slip into a coma. For four weeks, I visited him in the hospital every day, watching him lay there and wishing and praying he would not survive. I was a scared little girl who knew his passing was a way for the abuse to stop and didn't know of any other ways at that time. When he eventually passed away, I secretly always felt that I caused it through manifestation, by wishing, praying, and wanting him to leave. The abuse from him may have ended with his death, but the abuse continued in my life for a long time in the way I treated myself and relationships which mirrored my familiar childhood *emotional home.*

I tried to escape the unprocessed feelings from my childhood and learned that anything that numbed the emotional pain was temporary, followed by even more inner turmoil and pain. I never cried after my father's death as I didn't know how to express my emotions and talk about my feelings. I remember being so afraid of him and at the same time angry for the pain he caused me, my mom, and sister. I was also angry at myself for not being able to protect my mother, sister, or myself from him.

I've heard it said, *"Don't quit five minutes before the miracle,"* and some moments felt like there would never be light again. I experienced hopelessness and despair and am so grateful that God didn't take me from this earth when I no longer wanted to be here, but instead gave me the will and desire to get up another day & take another step. After wiping my eyes, I was able to see rays of hope peeking through the clouds and knew that there was more for me to do in my life.

Through years of soul searching, healing, and accepting love and support from others, I grew to have compassion for my dad, knowing he did the best he could with the emotional resources he had, as he too came from a home of physical abuse as a child. I discovered an unconditional love for him, not for what he did or didn't do for me, but just for his being and his true essence. I believe this divine essence is who we *really* are, before, during and after our time on earth. This pure essence is love and doesn't come with human flaws, as it is the soft perfection of our souls.

Additionally, I realized my childhood memories and stories around him, didn't serve me or anyone else and I *could* create a new story—one of forgiveness—letting him rest in peace while empowering me to feel unconditional love for another human being. To truly heal, I needed to also acknowledge him for the positive influences he contributed to my life. One did not exist without the other. My dad provided for our family financially and went from a Milkman to a successful Real Estate Broker. Consciously or unconsciously, his work ethic impressed upon me and my life in a positive way. I also believe my desire to learn Martial Arts was a result of my childhood feelings of vulnerability and lack of protection—I wanted to be able to take care of myself. I was no longer a *victim,* but rather a *victor* in my life to protect myself not just physically but also emotionally.

The word **Inspire** came to me at a motivational event, as a vision of a circular image with **Inspire** in the middle and rays of sunshine beaming from the center, representing all the different ways this could manifest into inspiring and helping others through my business and personal life. I truly understood what it was like to be smiling on the outside while crying on the inside and knew that many other people were living life the same way and I wanted to help others find hope and persevere to pursue their life dreams, no matter what and never give up.

My path is one of recovery, recovering from a state of mind that didn't serve me or others to one of inspiration, love, and a passion to help others. I dedicate my mornings to me and wake up at 4 a.m. to exercise, pray, meditate, read, write, and listen to something that feeds my mind and soul to help me grow. I respect the amount of energy I have for a given day and where I put that energy is up to me, including who I spend my time with, what I listen to, where I go and conversations I engage in, or choose not to. I surround myself with positive people, people that inspire and challenge me to grow. I attend motivational and personal development events, which continually push me out of my comfort zone and grow in all areas of my life.

Living in the moment also helps me appreciate my life even more. When I'm in nature hiking or running, I love to stop and use all my senses in that moment, really seeing the outline of the leaves on the trees and the details of the branches, the shapes of the clouds in the sky, hearing the birds & squirrels playing and rustling through the woods, smelling the clean air and knowing I will look back on this exact moment as fleeting, *never* to be experienced again, and soaking up all that a *unique* moment has to offer. A moment in time becomes a day, week, month, year, and ultimately our lives. It is as if I feel I am stopping the rapid clock of life for even a moment to be present and appreciate a moment of my life. Experiencing my life as a human *be*-Ing instead of always being a human *do*-Ing.

As this is a *journey*, I do not feel fulfilled and inspired every day, but I have faith in what I can't see, and a knowingness that "*this too shall pass.*" I believe life is happening *for me* and not *to me*. The difficult times in my life, have become a blessing and a beautiful gift. I have a sincere compassion and understanding for others who have experienced feeling hopeless because of their past. My inner peace and happiness are no longer contingent upon people, places, or things being a certain way. I am free to be the person God created me to be. I am not the same person I was yesterday, nor the one I will be tomorrow. Every day is an opportunity to be a little bit better version of myself from yesterday, not denying the past, but taking action steps every day to improve myself.

I aspire today to live in better alignment with my highest authentic self. I release anything that holds me back and feed my soul every day with healthy choices to nourish my mind, body, and spirit into a fulfilled and happy life.

I hope my story can inspire you to realize that no matter what yesterday was like or previous challenges you've had, it can be your greatest gift. You *do* matter, you are uniquely special, and your gift is **your** gift. Gifts are for giving, who will you inspire today with your gift? Spread your angelic wings and leave sparkles of your light to everyone you meet, and an unforgettable legacy of love. For in the end, love wins, heals, and conquers all.

Rhonda Alderman is an adventurous free-spirit and loves to live her life and every moment to the fullest. She enjoys dancing, hiking, running and kickboxing. Rhonda is passionate about travel and loves to explore new places while meeting beautiful new souls along the way. She is most proud of her two awesome sons and cherishes the special friendship she has with her beautiful mom. Rhonda is a Second-Degree Black Belt in Shorinji Kempo and trained in Japan Town, San Francisco, CA as well as in Japan. She jumped out of 800+ perfectly good airplanes for fun, specializing and competing in Freestyle Aerial Gymnastics Skydiving. Professionally, she is a Top Real Estate Realtor/Broker Associate in Sonoma County, California, and CEO of Inspire Capital Investments, Multifamily Apartment Investing.

Thank you, God & Angels, for your love and guidance to share this story from my heart. #111, #333, #444

www.RhondaAlderman.net
www.InspireCapitalInvestments.com

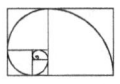

Riley Thomas

Dammit, He's Trying

My mom asked me a question, years ago now, when I first began confidently telling my family how I wished to be referred to: "What does it mean to be a man?" It was asked in a longer request, but all I really remember is the *question*. And my reaction. I couldn't answer it; hell, I don't think I could if I were asked today, but I remember it made me so angry. Visceral and vitriolic, I *hated* that question; it kept me up for weeks. That single question became this frustrating, festering ball of *something* that couldn't quite catch the light enough to be identified. This…reminder that no one could see what I did. That not a single person in that moment fully understood, maybe couldn't even grasp the idea that this wasn't a *decision*; it was just how things had always been. It's innate, as natural as breathing, as natural as telling your parents you love them when you leave the house. I don't have to explain why it's nice to be told I'm loved by my family. Why should I need to explain why it's nice to be gendered correctly?

I've struggled with that question for a long time. I've reckoned with it, bargained with it, taken lesser labels, swapped them out a month later when I still felt uncomfortable in my skin. I changed my pronouns from He/Him to He/They, gave people leniency, stopped taking it so hard when people misgendered me. But none of it has quieted that singular whisper, that one question: *"What does it mean to be a man?"*

It asked for an expression, an external measure of my masculinity. As it turns out, expression is my hairiest subject. I never insisted on wearing boy clothes, but I desperately held onto the memories of people "mistaking" me for a little boy at the supermarket. I liked my crown of bows, and I always liked being pretty; but I cried when I realized *why* I was being told to wear so many.

I never had a word for any of this, and it was never so pressing that I named it; but does something really need to be expressed to exist? My mom always points out how I never acted very traditionally masculine as a kid, and to that I raise you: I don't act very traditionally masculine now. I'm a queer neurodivergent trans native. Do you think anything about me is going to live up to the Western tradition?

I walked through life for years, looking for alignment and ignoring that icky feeling I got when people were perceiving me. I walked through life making others happy, making myself happy, but never feeling whole. Now I can look back and realize that icky feeling, that awful discomfort, was misalignment. Not in myself, not in my body, but with how people saw me.

I've always loved being a pretty boy. Why did it feel so bad for people to just see me as pretty?

I've learned how to describe my identity, how I feel about myself and the world around me—not out of a desire to express them to people, but out of the necessity to be understood. I've carved out my own spaces of comfort, tiptoed around other people's comforts. I've changed entire formats on how I introduce myself just to keep others happy. I've lived every single day choosing how to present myself to people. I've assessed safety, I've assessed interest, and the likelihood of being brushed off in favor of the more chill, less weird kids. I've learned to listen, learned to glean the context for a joke, learned to people watch because no one was willing to tell me what was happening. I've made allowances for other people, and I've forced allowances for myself. None of it, not a single step, brought me closer to the alignment I wanted, that I craved but couldn't name.

There's something polarizing about growing up always feeling like you need to explain what's happening in your head, why something makes you happy. It was never a feeling imposed by my family or those around me; it was rather something more background, more subconscious. This innate feeling that others wouldn't understand me—a feeling that's true scope has never been fully realized, that grows with every new corner to hide in that it discovers.

I can recognize, now, that the feeling is called *misalignment*, that this boogieman concept everyone always seems to talk about has seemingly affected me since before some of my earliest memories.

Recognizing, however, is very different from accepting. Accepting your misalignment is like accepting that what you've been seeing as blue is purple. It's sitting with the idea that what you've known for so long is wrong, that you've been missing this piece that everyone else has had their whole life.

Truly, though, no one is aligned by default. Finding alignment, this wonderful path everyone walks multiple times in life, is never easy for anyone. We all work to get there, just at different rates, with different convictions and speeds. Everyone is different, everybody is unique; those differences don't make us wrong, just human.

I believed for so long that I wasn't trans enough to talk about it, like my experience was too different from other trans men, that it would detract from their stories. But we all have the same similarity, a similarity that unites all people: Every single person is lost in a sea of misalignment, looking for that peace. Everyone is trying to explain, to express them-selves just as valiantly as I am.

I've realized fully, as of late, that my alignment is not just negatively decided by other people, that other people aren't my problem; they're just another variable in the bigger equation.

When I'm in a room full of people who respect me, who know me for who I really am, whatever misalignment was weighing on me fades into the background. I just need to be able to find those people. I have to recognize that I'm allowed to show people how to treat me, to give and withhold respect as it is given to me.

There's a peace that comes with those realizations, those acknowledgments. If I were a more poetic person, I'd try to make some beautiful anecdote out of how fitting it is to feel closer to alignment when recognizing your own misalignment; but I'm no poet, and life is never as clear as those people make it out to be anyway.

I am an obliger, a people pleaser as people like to say. I've never seen it as a bad thing necessarily, just another piece that made me who I am. No amount of anxiety or misalignment will ever be enough to change the fact that I care so deeply about people; but caring deeply about people doesn't mean allowing anxiety and misalignment. I am who I am, and who that is will change and shift just as my own alignment will. I do know one thing for certain: I don't live for anyone else, so why would I sacrifice my own expression, my own alignment, for them?

As much as I can say all of this, write some profound words about alignment and misalignment and my past experiences with it, in the eyes of a seventeen-year-old trans guy, what is alignment?

I feel like I really didn't have an answer until this past week. I hadn't truly sat down and thought it over, slowed down and observed alignment in my daily life, until I was asked to write about it. But what I found was almost…disappointing. There was nothing profound. There was no balanced yin-yang of alignment and misalignment. Alignment is coveted as much as it is shared; it's savored just as it is taken for granted. But none of that truly means anything when you step back and just watch. When you just live, when you just experience—those are the most aligned moments you can have.

Alignment simply…is. It permeates everything, flows in and out and through the best and worst moments of life. Alignment is not a positive any more than misalignment is a negative. Alignment is found in simply learning to live, to be comfortable. Alignment is found in learning to let go, learning that you don't need to control everything.

I know that one day in the future, I'll look in the mirror and be uncomfortable. Whether that is with who I am inside, outside, projected, internalized…it will happen. And when it does, I will do my best to welcome this misalignment with open arms, and then patiently await my newest alignment to sweep everything up once again.

▼ ▼ ▼ ▼ ▼

Riley Thomas was born December 2004, and is finally finding comfort in who he is. Navigating rough formative years, stolen adolescence, and postponed high-school experiences, he's learning that his past doesn't define him, nor do his differences. He's making an effort to take things easier, and to care less about what others think. There's a long way to go, but dammit, he's trying. Slowing down, just being a seventeen-year-old highschooler, is a lot. A son, a brother, a chicken dad. Worrying about attending his tribe's college, or what job he'll take over the summer. Small worries, peaceful concerns. Because he deserves to be a teenager, and to live life happily, fully in alignment.

"Get honest
with YOU.
More honest.
More than
that, even."

— Mistilei

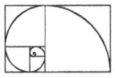

Tammy Thomas

Fat, Forty, and Female

How to Lose Your Limitations

Alignment is the story of a forty-year-old, 260-pound, mother and wife who walked into a gym on Main Street in her small hometown and ended up a fifty-year-old, 135-pound, #1 Amazon International Best Selling author and successful health and wellness coach helping many people change their lives and find their dreams.

It all started in 2012. My youngest child was starting pre-K. It was time for me. I began looking for a job close to home. I did not find too many options. Retail was not what I was looking for. I was driving down Main Street when I saw a "Now Hiring" sign in the window of a gym. I stopped, went in, and asked about the job. The job they posted on the sign for was not for me; it was for trainers and membership sales.

I noticed this gym had a smoothie bar and a kitchen. I asked the owner about serving healthy breakfast and lunch options. I convinced him to give me a chance. Over the weekend I created a healthy turkey sandwich with an avocado spread. I sourced the ingredients. I made the sandwiches, and I went around my small town giving out samples with a copy of my first menu. It was a hit. The restaurant was born. I cooked full meals from small kitchen appliances: an electric skillet, a rice cooker, a slow cooker, a convection oven, and a roaster. I had a full menu. I built a small following of regular customers. I was beginning to attract investors and met with a couple for dinner who were interested in acquiring a bigger, better location for my new restaurant.

Then the fire happened. It was a house fire. I got the call from my twelve-year-old daughter while I was at the gym restaurant. That call changed my life. I went straight home. The fire was out. The children were safe. My husband was safe but rattled and pacing. The county sheriff came to the house and asked for permission to search our home. We said, "Yes, we have nothing to hide." Except my husband had a small amount of cannabis on a tray in a dresser drawer. Cannabis was illegal in Oklahoma in 2012. We both went to jail for possession of drugs and drug paraphernalia, maintaining a home where drugs were sold and kept, and child neglect. It would take years to overcome the false charges and put our lives back together. Our children were removed from our custody and taken to my mother's on December 21, 2012. My husband and I went to jail. We were there for twenty days before we were able to plead guilty and get released. When we were released, we were homeless, childless, and abused *but not broken.*

We began the slow process of rebuilding. This is where alignment comes in. Alignment for me is a feeling, a voice, a knowing. I went back to the gym, like that's where I was supposed to be. I had no idea why. Fat, forty, and female does not scream gym employee, but I knew a healthy restaurant was needed in my little town. I felt compelled to start one. To be the change I wanted to see.

Then, in August of 2013, I went back to jail for *failure to pay.* That is the most ridiculous sentence. I went to jail. I was locked up. I had no way to contact anyone. But I made the most of it. I was selected to work in the sheriff's office the last few months I was there. Working made the time go by faster. I could make phone calls while I was at work. I talked to my husband every day. I had no one else to call. In January 2014 I was released for good behavior. Steve came to pick me up. I barely recognized the person who came to get me. He no longer looked and felt like I remembered.

The gym was now a dungeon. The office and kitchen were completely closed. Members were mostly gone. I began cleaning up the mess. A week later I started a membership drive and sold almost one hundred memberships in the first two months. I started running the personal training program in several locations in Northeast Oklahoma and three locations in Florida. Steve managed the Tulsa location of the same gym.

Steve and I were invited to Unleash the Power Within (UPW) in 2014, and my life has never been the same. I am fully aligned with health wellness and self-improvement. I am here to show others the way.

After walking on fire in October of 2014, I made some decisions. I would no longer accept the $3.14 an hour plus commission I was being paid when we left for UPW Dallas that Thursday morning. When I got back to the gym I reassessed my worth. I decided my many managerial duties did not leave me much time for sales. I was in a small town. That alone limited my sales prospects. I had to make a decision. I left in April.

Now what? It didn't matter. I was worth much more than half the normal minimum wage. I heard and listened to what Tony Robbins told me at UPW. I burned the boats. We moved to a new town. We found a gig doing property preservation. We did a little bit of everything, including mowing lawns, winterizations, lock changes, plumbing repairs, and installing appliances. We single-handedly completed rehabs of big, beautiful homes.

I spent most of my available moments on self-improvement. I joined the available Tony Robbins groups. I found new high-frequency friends. I found alignment with these high achievers and the groups they lead. I was not alone. There were people like me. I found YouTube. I found books. The doctors and speakers on YouTube became my friends. I was learning constantly. I was releasing the extra weight as I let go of my limitations. I was letting go of the pain. My husband and I were in and out of alignment—mostly in. If we had not been in alignment with our growth mind set, I would not have been able to grow into the beautiful human I am today.

We were homeless for a few weeks; now we own a house on the hill, and my children have come home. By the time we owned our own home, the judge ruled that their grandma was the abuser and that our children were coming home. We never abused our children, and it was so wonderful to have them back with us. We spent most of our time loving our children. We have spent the last few years simply being, growing, learning, and healing as much as possible. A huge amount of healing has taken place. My children are my joy. They are intelligent, eloquent, and genuinely good people. They went back to brick-and-mortar school this year. They are in a wonderfully supportive school. They are enjoying friends and a social life. It has been fun.

Wait a minute! I left out eight years, from 2014 to 2022. I now weigh 135 pounds, and I am a happy, healthy, vibrant woman ready to assist with the changes needed to find alignment. I am in alignment. I have been able to maintain my alignment with my high-frequency friends. I have attracted and aligned with some amazing people and opportunities. I get paid to help people live their best lives. I have helped people make the alignment changes to leave their unhappy marriages and subsequently find their soulmates. I am now the muse for those wanting to lose hundreds of pounds. I get the pleasure of watching people live their dreams. There is nothing that makes me happier than knowing I can be the voice that helps others.

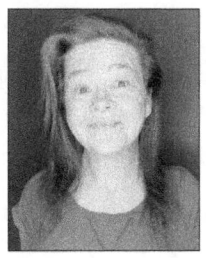

Tammy Thomas is a fifty-year-old mother of five, an observer, a giver of wisdom, beauty, and love, and a healer, nurturer, and loving soul. An accomplished cook and winner of recipe contests, she is co-owner of House on the Hill Produce and Bakery. She owns Reflections Life Health and Wellness, and is the creator of Women Unite. Abuse happens at all ages and takes many forms. Even when the direct abuse ends, the effects remain. We have a responsibility to abused women and children to help them break free of the cycle. It is not their fault they are being or have been abused, and that they don't know there are alternatives or haven't been shown how to carry on and build something beautiful when they finally break free. It is the fault of society allowing it to happen, of each of us turning our heads for fear of getting involved and being glad it isn't us. Tammy's commitment is that from this day forward it *will not* be our fault that there is no support when—and long after—they've decided they are worth loving. The most important job she has is to continue healing out loud. Because of Tammy, she hopes others can find their way to the light.

www.facebook.com/tammy.inmanthomas
www.instagram.com/tammygg33/?next=%2F
www.youtube.com/channel/UCJZMxe6ADNI70MbG_wV7WMA

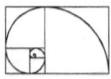

Sharon Wible

Reaching Through the Veil

Life has a convoluted way of gifting us with sublime experiences one moment, then robbing us of them the next. I went to bed one August evening as my husband's wife and friend, and woke up a widow. Jim's sudden death propelled me into a spiral of grief. I kept waiting to be pulled from this world and into his because together is where we needed to be. Living without him was unimaginable, yet the days relentlessly pummeled onward. Every day I thought would be my last, but I kept waking up morning after morning, physically and emotionally stuck.

After a couple of months, life went on for everyone else; however, mine remained stagnant. I needed guidance, so I met with Theresa, my counselor I trusted from the past who had helped me through life's inevitable challenges. Theresa suggested making changes to my daily routine. I was still trying to replicate the habits of the lives we shared because it felt like *us*, but I was now a *me*. I needed to change my day, but I didn't know how to do it. The cold, dark winter was creeping up on me quickly as October neared its end, and I still didn't feel much better. My core purpose for the past few decades had been to raise my children and take care of my husband. Now that core purpose no longer existed.

Theresa suggested I sign up for an evening class at the local community college. Being a teacher, I love learning, and I love school, so it seemed to be a sound decision. I signed up for a personal development class called Developing Intuition. This was a monumental event for me. I was a swirl of emotions and nerves. I needed assurance it would go as smoothly as possible. I didn't know what to expect of the class or of myself. Would I even be able to get out of my car? Could I walk through the door of the classroom without crumbling?

I pulled into the lot and parked under a lamppost. The sign on it read "Q." That was a lot to recall. I wrote "Q" on the front of my notebook so, like a trail of breadcrumbs, I could find my way back to my car. Methodically, I lifted myself out of the car, threw my purse onto my shoulder, and grabbed my notebook from the passenger seat. I crossed the lot and stepped up onto the walkway, which led to the building that I'd found earlier on the map. I entered through the glass doors, traveled up the stairs, and walked through the threshold of the classroom.

The instructor, Rhonda, was a slight woman dressed in a violet sweater and ebony dress slacks. A woolen shawl loosely draped her shoulders. A golden chain dangled a pendant of a rooted tree, which swung just above her stomach as she moved about behind a table. Her smile was contagious as I stepped into the class. Her voice was soft and wispy as she smiled and said, "Hello, hello. Welcome," gesturing with her slender hand for me to find a place to sit. The tables, arranged in a horseshoe, were inviting. I sat down by a lady who was already chatting with the woman beside her. A few more people slowly filled the room. Everyone was quiet but smiled at one another. I set up my notebook, pen, and my bottle of water.

After taking attendance and reviewing some obligatory housekeeping information, Rhonda introduced herself and welcomed us. She then led the class with a short guided meditation. She turned off the lights, and we closed our eyes, relaxed our bodies, and cleared our minds, Rhonda's hypnotic, soft voice leading us through. I left my stresses of the day at the door, breathing in slowly and releasing tension. I felt deep within me that this was where I needed to be. When we were ready, we opened our eyes.

I was delighted by the diversity of our group: a young man from India who had just recently moved to the United States, a young college student wearing a silver nose ring, an artist, a business major, a generously tattooed man celebrating his one-year sobriety, two ladies in their seventies who had been friends since grade school, and me, a recently widowed woman digging her way out from grief while searching for purpose. We were all so different, but we all freely embraced one another. There was peace and ease in the room. Everyone seemed to be so accepting of one another, so the environment felt safe.

After the introductions, Rhonda explained the first exercise we were to practice was to develop awareness of our intuition. The exercise was to feel the energy and become aware of our partner's intention. The seated partner would set an intention of either focusing energy going within or energy pulling outward. It was a choice, but it was not to be shared with the other partner. The other partner was to stand behind the seated partner and intuitively feel the direction of the energy.

I partnered with Kylie, the young college student with the nose ring. She was an old soul, thoughtful, patient, and totally taken with the exercise. Rhonda suggested to the class that we find a different classroom or hallway where we could focus. Before beginning the exercise, we were to first breathe and settle ourselves. Kylie and I found a classroom across the hall and began. I volunteered to sit down first. We settled ourselves through breathing as Rhonda suggested.

With what little energy I had, I focused inward. I turtled into my darkness and avoided going outside myself. My initial reaction, then, was to focus my energy inward as deeply as it could go, but then I suddenly saw Jim in my mind, smiling at me! He wore a sparkling white t-shirt, and his skin was tanned like autumn caramel. He looked incredibly handsome, his face as youthful as it was when we first met. He took my breath away. I felt his arms resting gently around my waist, shaking me ever so slightly, wanting me to hear his message: *You have so much love in you, and you need to give it away. You can't keep it. All the love you have for me now has to go out to others.* So I changed my focus…for him. I envisioned an electric indigo light streaming out of me. I adjusted my shoulders back and down. I felt strong. I concentrated on pushing out my unseen energy. And I breathed.

My hands were cupped gently together on my lap as I continued breathing and focusing on the intense blue light, when I felt something drop into my hands. I opened my eyes and looked down. My butterfly necklace, which nestled a portion of my husband's cremains, had fallen into my hands. I wore it every day to physically carry Jim with me. I rarely exposed it, keeping it safe inside my shirts and sweaters. It was more intimate for me that way. At first I assumed that the clasp had broken and was so grateful that I hadn't lost it. I set my necklace on the ledge of the whiteboard until the exercise was finished. Kylie and I changed placement and repeated the exercise. Both of us identified our energy correctly; mine went outward and hers went inward.

Before putting it into my jeans pocket, I looked at the clasp. Nothing was broken. Suddenly, my knees gave way, and the ledge of the white-board caught my fall. The Universe had miraculously allowed the veil to fall for a brief moment as Jim and the Divine connected with me, encouraging me to dig my way out from under the anvil of grief and to begin to rise out of myself. I listened to him and to my intuition, and I was blessed with an affirmation. My necklace falling into my lap was a divine intervention. It had never before, nor has it since, fallen from around my neck. Meditation, stillness, and intention allowed me to connect with the spiritual, the invisible, the truth. Jim encouraged me that night to move forward. Jim literally fell into my lap that evening.

Grief has now rewired my spiritual development. As the widow's fog slowly lifted, I became aware of the impermanence of the world around me. The relationships with those I cherish will end. The possessions and the stuff could be taken from me at any time. This world will end, as will my body, but my spirit will live on; there is no birth, there is no death. There is only *is*…timeless and present.

Death is only sad when you're on the living side of it. I don't know what the rest of my life will entail, but I must turn what I have into enough. I alone am enough.

▼ ▼ ▼ ▼ ▼

Sharon M. Wible is an insatiable reader and avid writer. She holds degrees in English and social studies and a master's degree in instruction and curriculum. Sharon currently teaches eighth grade American history and is nearing completion of her first children's book. Sharon's writing journey began after the sudden passing of her husband, Jim. After reading numerous books written by those who experienced trauma, she discovered there can be life after loss. Sharon found her own voice and transformation through her years of writing and reflecting. She created *StoryLight*, her blog discussing grief and healing. It is not *if* loss happens, but *when* it happens, so sharing our stories builds a community of resilience, strength, and hope. Sharon's interests include traveling, gardening, running, and kickboxing. Sharon's greatest joys are her children and grandchildren. She resides in a quiet suburb in Imperial, Missouri, with her silly goldendoodle, Phoebe.

www.sharonmwible.com/
www.sharonmwible.com/my-books
www.linkedin.com/in/sharon-wible-6a7352218/
www.instagram.com/sharonwible/

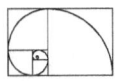

Steve Hudgins

Thankful for a Glass

As a child, I was fascinated with ants, how hard they work in their community, and how quickly they adapt and overcome threats to their colony. They wander into areas with a sense of purpose to collect food for their well-established community. When there is a derailment, they communicate quickly and effectively to establish a new sense of order. Ants march with meaning and are aligned in a row with intent and purpose to obtain their ultimate goal.

It's Monday, like any "moan day" that can appear intimidating after a quiet, lazy weekend of fun. The alarm sounds, awakening the soldier within to a sense of purpose: time to start the week. The sleep of the eye is wiped away, the open cave of a yawn expands, and limbs are stretched to stimulate the body and alert the mind, "It's time to get going." Yet this morning, something is off. My legs feel like concrete as my feet shuffle into the bathroom to prepare for the day.

I pause to consider whether or not things appear normal; then a feeling comes over me. It's as if a wind comes out of nowhere, and, in the quiet of the morning, the shutters start to shake. I feel a stirring within my body that is not normal. *I wonder if the ants feel the shake of large feet tramping around their community.* The storm begins, and I try to stay on track, but I foretell there is a derailment ahead.

Having not been prepared for that disruption, I went to the office and met with a client but soon knew I should cancel the rest of my morning clients. I felt an urgency to go to the emergency room because of the onset of rigors—a medical term for uncontrollable shivering due to a high fever. My instinct kicked in as my body started trembling. I was shaking as if I were cold, but there was no cold to be felt.

I left the normalcy of the office behind, determined to find out what was happening to me. Something was seriously off. I wondered if I was like an ant getting confused when its ammonia trail is sprayed with bleach. *Where's the right track?*

Although confused, I was able to call the Veterans Health Administration clinic. I got anxious when I was told that the nurse could not take my call because they were too busy. Finally, I was transferred to the triage nurse, who advised me to immediately get to the emergency room. As a well-trained military soldier, I followed the order. Also, I felt unsafe and at risk.

There was an emergency room at a nearby civilian hospital. Huffing across the parking lot and trying to control the shaking, I knew I was about to crash, but I made it inside and successfully landed on the chair in front of the intake triage nurse. What I hoped would be a quick catch and release ended with me being admitted to the hospital after labs revealed there was too much troponin in my blood. All I knew was that my heart kept searching for normal rhythms, seeking alignment.

What started at 0930 left me parched and hungry, as I'd had no breakfast, lunch, or dinner. I was handed and felt thankful for a glass of chipped ice, its slow melt down my throat quenching my thirst. It calmed my spirit. I knew a calm mind would help me recover more quickly so I could get back on track. But I sensed another shoe was about to drop. It happened at 0100 on Tuesday in my private room. The rigors were so strong that it was as if I were exploding from the inside out, like a violently shaken soda. My normal breathing turned into hyperventilating. I heard a code on the intercom for room 409, my room, and twelve nurses appeared. Then suddenly, nothing.

Three hours later, I came to, completely disoriented. As my eyelids slowly lifted, I felt like I was raising blinds to let the sunlight in. My room was different, like I had fallen through a black hole and awakened in a new world. But it was just the intensive care unit. The nurses explained that I almost died of a severe reaction to septic shock. Feeling as if I were in shark-infested waters, I found out three different types of bacteria were simultaneously attacking my body. The doctors called me an enigma. No one knew how or why I derailed into septic shock. My body was out of alignment, but my spirit and emotional state stayed balanced.

A brand-new day began. I'll fast-forward like a DVR recording to save you from the mundane details. I began to stabilize after they pumped antibiotics into me every eight hours. I only had ice chips because they planned to take me to surgery. I hadn't had any solid food or IV drips since Monday. Another glass of ice chips kept me grounded and grateful for what I had.

On Wednesday at 0200, the nurse, Michelle, came into my room to give me my medications. She looked at me and asked, "Would you like to get cleaned up?"

I replied, "Yes, because I am like a fish, and after three days I can tell there is a smell." She chuckled and went to get the supplies.

The warmth of water and shampoo on my hair was refreshing, and I embraced my renewed fragrance. While dressing and regaining my sense of dignity, the voice of Oz spoke behind the curtain: "number five is about to pass." *I was puzzled and wondered if there were something that should be done to prepare for someone dying.*

Michelle explained softly that an eighty-one-year-old woman had been admitted to the ICU on July 1, 2022. I heard her empathy as she explained that #5 did not have family, friends, or visitors to come and see her. Michelle had to leave me to go sit with the woman, to hold her hand, so she would not drift all alone into the other side as her soul passed from the temporal to the eternal.

I thought of my family dispersed throughout Oklahoma and Texas. My grandson's third birthday was coming that Saturday, and I wanted to surprise them with my presence in Denton, Texas. During the forty minutes of silence while the nurse was gone from my room, my mind whirled with what-ifs. Being so unsettled affected me in ways I could not fathom. I felt despair hover over me like a blanket of fog.

Michelle came back with puffy eyes. She had removed her white sweatshirt. Looking up at her, I acknowledged with sincerity and empathy that she should take some time for herself and not worry about me. As a clinician myself, I could tell she needed a recharge.

Alone again, I wondered how I would be able to bring my body back into alignment after this. The passage my body went through made my emotions shift, and I sensed the opening of hope after the darkness I'd surrendered to on Monday.

As a faith-based person, I felt a peacefulness about all of this that gave me a sense of security and wonder. *The valley that is walked is defined by the reaction we allow. The valleys are filled with learning if the lesson is received.* My journey through the dark-shadowed valley was shortened when I accepted the pain of derailment by acknowledging, confronting, and embracing it. If I hadn't chosen to accept it and instead chose not to engage, deny the pain, or refuse to address it, I would have stayed in the valley. Ignoring or denying it does not remove pain. To align my mind involves understanding there will always be pain, but it is how receptive I am to make the transition that determines my ability to thrive.

Accepting derailments and distractions and finding opportunities to stay aligned is essential. I must anticipate what will happen next, having learned from the pain. *I again wonder about the ants who remain on the path even when there is a distraction because they have a sense of community, but it's more than that.* I've learned alignment is not reacting and controlling as ants do. It is about becoming aware, so I consciously manage change with clear intentions and a generous purpose. There's my clarity? I am being called to build a sense of community knowingly and intentionally so I am never alone.

My faith in a Creator helped me peacefully realign. People have expressed that a glass half full is optimistic, and a glass half empty is pessimistic. My near-death experience gave me a healing attitude that helped me stay aligned. *I am thankful to have a glass. Without it, whatever is poured into my life would be lost.*

▼ ▼ ▼ ▼ ▼

Steve Hudgins, MA, LPC-S, NCC, is a licensed professional therapist working on a doctoral degree from Liberty University. As a military veteran, a cancer survivor, a former engineer, and a former director of an inpatient hospital, he overcame a 34 percent chance of living to 2021 due to a cancer diagnosis in 2018. He is now living a healthy life. His counseling practice is in a town east of Tulsa, Oklahoma. The combination of work experiences and life experiences have enabled him to help others who have gone through complex challenges. He hosts a weekly podcast, *Coached Soul*, designed to help listeners become "a better you" by interviewing people whose stories reveal surviving a low point and finding redemption. His battles have made him a therapist who can sympathize and empathize with a proper understanding of what others are going through.

www.prcounseling.com
www.coachedsoul.com
steve@prcounseling.com

"Magic is only
as abundant
as you allow."

— Mistilei

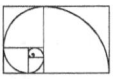

Amy Nicastro-Clark

Allowance vs. Resistance

Allowing myself to have the life I deserve was not easy. It has been a journey to my soul. Life has been the best and worst roller coaster, not in any order. I spent my youth running hard from feeling too much, then too little, and then grew to not feel at all. The past few years have taught me how to be alive and that I want to feel everything. We learn way too late that life is about the relationships we make, not the money we make. Money can't buy love, for ourselves or for anyone else. Unconditional love for ourselves will allow us to love others. How I treat myself is how I treat everything. The healing space I am creating will teach others to do the same.

Our families are a gift to our existence when we are open to seeing the gift. Our journey is our own. It's not about "he did this" or "she did that." It's how we choose to get to know ourselves, love ourselves, celebrate ourselves, and it's all a practice. Growing up in the sixties in a divorced family was hard. I thought we were the only ones. My parents were children when they married—my father twenty-two, and my mother nineteen—two people with ideals of making babies to give them what they never had. Children think parents are gods, and they are, and are not.

As an empath with curly hair no one could brush, I was different from all my siblings. I thought there was something wrong with me, really wrong with me. My brain moved fast and I had no idea how to slow it down. The teasing I received, like most kids in a big family, didn't help. My reactions were great entertainment, so teasing continued for years. I took it very personally, even when it wasn't, and my mother didn't stop them. I could not wait to have children and treat them the way I wanted to be treated.

My father was my hero. He did his best to stop the teasing by removing me from the situation. The four little ones spent weekends with him, and I got to go to work with him. He gave me purpose. The middle of six, I grew up between my brothers. They taught me my competitive edge. I wanted to be a quarterback. Sports were my everything. I am an athlete, and I had to be good at sports to have fun. My brothers not only got my father's expertise; they also got the expertise of the neighborhood fathers who coached. I wanted to be happy for them, and I wanted so badly to be a boy. I would have done anything. I cried, pulled my hair out, and was so unhappy. My father saw my frustration and taught me a sport my brother's didn't play: basketball. I fell in love and was good. I believed in myself playing basketball. I got picked for the boys' teams after school, at the park—not last. I grew up when girls did not get to play organized sports, which led me to other ways to satisfy myself.

Education came easy, and I was bored in high school. My entrepreneurial spirit started then, making a business out of helping my friends feel good and getting high for free. It started with pot and grew into other things. I fell in love young, in high school, with a boy who looked like Hercules. He was funny, and thinking of him made my body smile. Being with him made me want to work out every day and appear thinner than him when we walked together down the hallway. Latching on to him, I expected him to make me happy—a big responsibility for any kid. We didn't know how to make ourselves happy.

I found a love that served my loneliness, and we started doing things we should not have been doing and got pregnant. I was fifteen, excited. It was a dream come true, although short lived. My mother stepped in to assure me I was not having a baby. She twisted my brain about my boyfriend and established that under no uncertain terms was she raising my baby. We aborted the baby, and a piece of me died too. This started my spiral. I couldn't handle it, and neither could my mother. She sold our family home a year or so later, taking my baby sister with her. I stayed, and it felt like I'd abandoned her. I beat myself up with drugs that led me away from my boyfriend and on to harder drugs. Heroin became my drug of choice. It numbed me. I am very lucky to be here to share the story.

One day, the Universe knocked. I saw Mike Barnicle on Chronicle. I had just gotten high at my friend's house. She'd helped me, as I would not stick needles in my own arm, so I went last most of the time. This beautiful summer day, I was patiently waiting and watching television. Chronicle was playing with Mike Barnicle on Sonoma Street in Dorchester, Massachusetts, interviewing the person who stood at the door of the shooting galleries, a place junkies could go and use clean needles and get high. AIDS was just entering the scene. The man at the door benefited with heroin they shared for the use of the clean needles. There I was, sitting stoned, in great physical shape because I worked out every day. I had my roller skates on, which were my means of transportation at the time. The Universe was so good to me that day. The man he interviewed had open sores the length of his thigh and was asked what they were from. He replied that they were from the cut in the heroin he shot. I was shocked. My first thought was, "I will never shoot heroin again. I will only shoot Dilaudid or Demerol." I became a careful junkie.

That man had a huge role in saving my life. I started to notice things and people. I saw my father coming down our long driveway one day, getting old, salt and pepper around his ears. It's when I said in my head, "Geez, I never thought I would grow up to be a junkie." I made a conscious decision to stop the needles. I began to detox myself with Percocet, five a day, two in the morning and three at night. Then I wanted to stop. Never are people more giving than when you're looking to stop. I would say "I quit," and my friends would hand me five for free. To get clean, I left my circle of friends and got closer to my Dad. Most of my friends did not live. My father invested a lot of money into my healing therapies. He believed in me.

Hercules came back into my life after a life-threatening car accident that killed our best friend. We reunited, and I had the baby I'd always wanted. We married, and because he continued to struggle with alcohol, I decided to support him and join his sober living. His behavior saved my life. In 2000 I found out I had Hepatitis C. None of my three children were born with it, and had he and I been happily drinking, I would be dead. I have a mentor who's taught me that Life is ALWAYS happening for me, and not to me. His education and a daily priming exercise have shown me how to love myself.

Relationships are not easy, especially the one we have with ourselves. Happiness is an inside job. That can be a gift or a double-edged sword. Growing up is not automatic just because we have a birthday. Maturity must be involved, and it requires intention. When I became intentional about who I am in the world, my work began. I needed to find my femininity that I always thought was a weakness. I've attended a women's weekend, and I join circles of women once a week, which has helped melt the brick surrounding my heart. I've learned from other women how to melt the tomboy.

Apologizing to my mother over and over, life got lighter. I made my mother's life hard. Had I listened to her, I would not have gotten pregnant at fifteen, forcing her to make a decision she didn't want to make either. I needed to learn to love and trust myself first. Listening to what the universe has to offer has made a huge difference in my life. Investing in myself and surrounding myself with intentional givers from my Platinum family taught me that family lifts each other up. With faith over fear, my wall of protection could come down. I could trust myself. Following the signs that show me the way has brought me to my mission of healing. Our best friend is in the mirror, the image that carries our middle name. (What else could it be for? We rarely use it.) The message in the mirror is "we are never alone." We have ourselves to answer to. My competition now is to be a better version of myself.

The Universe has been knocking on my brain for years. Over the past few I have been able to hear it. Once I learned to be the best version of myself, I had to make myself number one. How I take care of myself is how I take care of everything. As the journey continues, I fight for my good habits. It's part of my game of life. That's my resistance. I had no idea how to feel happy as a child; it was foreign and uncomfortable. I would say the real test was committing to things that made me feel good inside. Exercise, meditation. A daily exercise of gratitude with my peers who have become my chosen family has been a game changer. My childhood crush and wasband is my friend, and I will always love and appreciate his strengths and weaknesses.

My vision of boosting morale while crossing the country in my thirty-two-foot camper to share my wisdom is coming. I am venturing into corporate America, school districts, and hospitals to share self-care, and to teach children how to love themselves first. Respect themselves first. To teach people that their body is a host for their soul and is a gift that needs care. Happiness is our own responsibility. My parents' only flaw was not teaching coping skills, which they couldn't because they didn't have them, nor did I. I am grateful to have become the best of both of them. As far as my hair, I have decided this is how the thoughts come out of my head, and sometimes I iron them out. What we resist persists.

To my reader, allow yourself the life you deserve by taking care of the gift you received. Life is a gift; you need to see it to have it.

Amy Nicastro-Clark is a serial entrepreneur and inventor who would give the world away. The lessons she has learned have taught her giving is the best drug there is, and that self-care is not selfish it is a necessary part of life to be successful in all our relationships, especially the one with ourselves. A native of Brookline, Massachusetts, she is the daughter of Cosmo D. Nicastro Jr. and Elizabeth Nicastro, two people who met very young and looked to live the American Dream by having child after child. Amy is one of five siblings and is grateful to all of them for teaching her resilience and strength, something she thought she could never have. Mother of three amazing adult children and Grammy of four (so far): Aidan, Jack, Lena, and Arlo. She is grateful to be a part of this amazing group of writers. A Platinum Partner of Tony Robbins, Amy just completed a year of amazing growth. She is here to share the wisdom. A healer at heart. Grateful for my Dream Team of Women.

Join mothers in the fight against addiction to save our children! Please donate using this link:
Fundraiser by Dar Walden : Mothers Against Addiction (gofundme.com)
If anyone would like to join this group, share this link: WhatsApp Group Invite
www.facebook.com/amy.n.clark.7

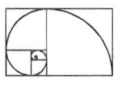

Ginine Mizerski

From Bullying to Bliss

The day I made up my mind

As I write this, I am resting in my lovely backyard sanctuary with my beautiful peach tree, azaleas, elephant ears, mint, mint, and more mint, and my saltwater pool. These were all things on my vision board from years past, and here I am basking in this peace, this joy. I am no longer afraid to step off the ledge and fly. I am no longer afraid to fail forward. I am no longer afraid to impact this world and unapologetically be my full, authentic *me*! I dance around my pool like no one is watching, with Fleetwood Mac exploding from my Bluetooth speaker. I love like there's no tomorrow and live in gratitude every single day. I look up to the gorgeous Texas sky and see the sun seeping through that one gray, half-white cloud with a ray of light—what I call a "Jesus sky"—and it speaks to me, saying, "Hello, I'm here. Take a little bit of my light, seek refuge, lay your head on my heaven pillow, and take in the love." It is amazing that I have learned to live in alignment and what that really means. However, let's be real. It has taken years of therapy, hard work, and learning how to fully transform my mind from the internal bully inside, which is my own worst enemy.

My life began in Pasadena, California, in November of '66. I guess it was a normal, typical upbringing. What wasn't normal was the constant pain inside. I struggled with cripplingly low self-esteem, depression, and constant lies in my head telling me I was worthless and not good enough. From early on, I combatted this with "doing" all the time. Being a high achiever was a way to earn my worth with my parents and prove it in this world.

I adored my mother and put her up on a pedestal. I also spent a lot of time waiting for my daddy to come home. He was gone a lot, often out of the country for work. I waited day after day for him, but when he was home he would sit on the couch or be in the garage, physically present but very far away. I didn't understand why he rarely smiled, rarely spoke to us. My heart was continually broken when he was around. I was too young to know he was in a constant state of depressive illness, drug and alcohol abuse. I often prayed he wouldn't come home so I didn't have to be sad seeing him the way he was.

One day, he never did come home. This moment would haunt me for many years to come. His body was found by a hiker at the bottom of a cliff deep in the mountains, weeks later. A murder investigation occurred that ended up being a cold case. During this time is when the truth about my father, my life, our whole existence started coming out. There was a lot kept from us. So many lies. Who was my father really? My father lived a double life. He worked for the government but also for the other side and was an addict and dealer.

Learning this shook me upside down and threw me sideways. But my mother was always our rock, and the best thing she did was take us away from Southern California to escape the pain and to follow rumors of a better life.

A couple years after moving, I went over the edge without hesitation. Until then I was any mom's dream child. Straight A student, no drugs, too nerdy (or insecure) to date. My mother didn't know at that time that my mind wasn't right. I hid it all too well. I learned early on how to wear masks. When I went over the edge, I put myself in some very dangerous and unhealthy situations. As a result, my relationship with my mother suffered some serious downs. I got into drugs, slept around, hung out with some shady, toxic people.

A few years later I was working at the Black Angus while going to college, holding a job at a bank, and singing in a jazz ensemble. (Do, do, do—are you getting the picture?) The bar/restaurant life is insane, and that's when I got into cocaine. I needed the energy to keep up all this "doing," or at least that is how I justified it. And on top of all the other crazy stuff, I was unknowingly keeping company with the infamous East Side Serial Killer (reserved for another story). But yes, the cops showed up at my day job and stated they believed I was next on his list. This man was still on the lam, and they placed me under immediate police protection. To say the very least, I was a mess from the inside out.

The night I got clean and decided I wanted to change, I was sitting in a dark, scary parking lot waiting for an acquaintance to bring me back my hundred dollars' worth of cocaine. There was a strange quiet around me. I thought about how this would break my mother's heart. Then a spirit whispered audibly into my ear, "Leave now and never go back." I made up my mind.

This began my journey out of the darkness. Music and God became my lifelines. I was created to sing and write songs. My passion and purpose, I believe, is to impact the world and give a little hope through my music. And yes, music became therapy for me.

Fast-forward a couple decades, I have won awards for my songs, ministered in prisons/jails, churches, and bars. My songs are on TV, in ads and films. I've toured the world. Success is a funny thing, though, because I had it all on the outside, but inside I was suffering from deep lows and severe imposter syndrome. To be honest, I still didn't really know how to just *be*. The true enlightenment, the deep change, happened when I learned how to change my mindset and control my thoughts.

You see, in 2020 I fell into a deep abyss. My world had been turned upside down, as it was for many others. For me, it was because a lot of my "doing" was suspended. And I had been doing so much "doing" that my tank was empty. I was exhausted physically and emotionally. And my mind? My stinking thinking?

It took a combination of things to help me heal and get into alignment. Of course, the health regimen I was doing was essential, and I was resting. I found an amazing counselor. I read *Battlefield of the Mind* by Joyce Meyer, a book that changed my life. Each of these things were catalysts to true change and healing.

To go even further, I heard the voice again. This time it said, "Sell everything you own and move to Texas." I asked aloud, "Are you kidding? Did I hear you correctly?" No answer.

For two weeks I prayed, I fasted, I waited. Finally, I knew what I was going to do. I admit, it was difficult and sad to leave my mother behind in Washington. Especially because of her sad calls, and the one that, for a brief moment, threw me off my Zen cloud.

She said to me, "If it weren't for you kids, I would leave this earth. I want to die."

Let me put it in perspective. This woman could peel paint off the walls with her prayers and strength. She was a single mom of six, fighting for a better life for every one of us, but now she'd lost her purpose. Ever since my dad was killed, she'd been without a special someone to share the rest of her life. Having kids is fine; it's just not the same.

Hearing her say "I am worthless now. No good to this world" shook my universe. As an empath who takes on others' pain as my own, my mother's words made the ground beneath me crumble into dust and ash. But then I thought, "She's choosing *me*. She's being vulnerable with me. Right at this moment, I'm her special person." What a gift! What a joy.

I knew I needed to meet her in this place of vulnerability. I had the choice to ignore the fear and thoughts in my own head and listen deeply to her pain *without* taking it on as my own. I didn't need to say the perfect words or save her! As Jennie Allen states in her book, *Find Your People*, "Vulnerability is the soil for intimacy, and what waters intimacy is tears."

And oh, did we shed tears together. I showed up for her, which meant I was also in alignment with my true purpose. It wasn't about being perfect (and it certainly wasn't about me); it was about being present, listening, and just giving her my full attention. I even said a little prayer, asking for the Holy Spirit to guide me. I remember the conversation ended with a glimmer of hope. My mom was actually laughing. I could hear her smile through the phone. It was also progress for me, as I used to be crippled with depression after our calls.

It isn't always easy, and while I don't recognize the girl I was, I have returned to my innocent, trusting, and joyful child spirit, minus the negative, crippling thoughts in my head. By stopping the internal bullying, listening to spirit voice, and being present for others, I can make up my mind. I can catch myself and resume my best life by shifting from internal bullying to blissful realignment. I live in the light. Now that's transformation.

Ginine Emily (aka Lace & Grit) lives in Plano, Texas, with her three fur babies. Her mantra is "Grit it out, then lace it up." She is a singer, song-writer, music producer, mental health advocate, inspirational speaker, and podcast host of *Survivor of the Weird*. She shares her stories and songs across the world to inspire and bring hope to a hurting world. Ginine Emily is recognized by numerous music professionals as possessing unique and extraordinary vocal prowess and has performed with the Seattle band, Chasing Oz, and now with Hearts In Sync. You may also hear many of her songs on TV and film. She volunteers for her church and other outreaches and is a Texas state representative for Celebrate Recov-ery. She left the corporate world to pursue a life in alignment with her values and passions, which are loving people, God, and music, and helping women not just survive but be *overcomers*, free from fear and the chains that bind them so they may live authentic lives.

www.laceandgrit.com/contact
linktr.ee/ginineemily
heartsinsync.live

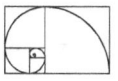

Kenya Evelyn

A Clean, Clear Channel

The year was 2002. I had just watched *The Secret*. Everything made sense in my body, as if it were an ancient truth, but nothing made sense in reality. I didn't understand how to manifest, how to create abundance, or how to achieve my dreams and purpose without fighting all the energies around me.

I remember vividly going through life with back pain and heartaches, accepting them as part of adulthood since "everyone has some kind of pain." I remember sleepless nights having to get clear on important decisions and feeling like my body was fighting my spirit, even though I didn't have this language. If you had asked me if I were in alignment, I would have looked at you like you had two heads. What does this even mean? And how do I know when I am in alignment?

I now think of alignment as a clean, clear channel that magnetizes the physical body, light body, ethereal body, and spiritual body all as one. It's the most incredible gift to embrace ourselves as magnets and powerful beings created to be one with God and to experience abundant life. Our very breath reveals the abundance of air as physical evidence that we have already been given everything we need to consummate our purpose in this world.

When I concentrate on my frequency, whatever intention I am holding becomes what is. It feels so good. I feel abundance as the frequency of God Himself. He is all possibility, all expansion, all overflowing. Scientists have decoded a message in our DNA that reads: *God Eternal within the body*. This makes so much sense to me, as we are children of God.

If you are still fighting with your spirit, it's because you aren't listening or feeling. You are not in tune with yourself. In this state, if financial abundance, for example, were to show up in your life, you wouldn't be able to experience fulfillment because it would be coming from a place of misalignment. This is because you have forgotten that everything in nature follows the law of abundance, and that we don't create abundance; we create limitations. We are nature, we are we, there is no separation. When we connect and align with our soul's mission and desires, we experience success, happiness, and love. We experience alignment.

We are always attracting or repelling. I still remember being in total hopelessness crying on the bathroom floor or in the shower so no one would hear me. I was so tired of experiencing life as an emotional roller coaster. One day it was great, the next day deep despair. I was feeling separated and powerless, asking God, "How in the world did I get here?"

Then I heard myself say, "You heal your relationships by healing yourself." Awareness went deep into my soul. I saw it as the ultimate gift of free will and choice, being aware of thoughts, actions, food, clothing, music, movies, friends…everything that influences me. So, how did I get here?

I came to Nashville single. I dreamed of having my music heard in all four corners of the world. Instead, I was facing childhood traumas, unable to trust myself, and feeling like I had made many decisions that didn't serve my purpose (so I thought), and, clearly, I had no one to blame. (I also had no idea that my mess was from generational frequencies running the show).

Questioning everything and everyone in my life, I felt self-hatred because of my choices. I was overweight, overworked, and overthinking. The voices in my head were so loud, there was no way I could hear my spirit. That was the moment life got even darker. I was feeling purposeless, and my health declined. I was constantly suffering severe migraines. It was like my soul screamed, "Stop!"

I truly believe that even when we are in our weakness, someone's prayers are reaching us; our angels are there whispering hope and resonating truth. I could feel the prayers of my mom and grandmother, which helped me carry on, even with many layers of brokenness. I had let myself go while I was doing and saying the right things for others, not being able to tune in to me.

I found out on social media that my grandmother had passed. She had raised me and my sister from birth, being the model of unconditional love for us. My uncle was watching over her in Brazil, and he made all the decisions for her burial without including any of us. When we found out, she was already under dirt. It was just a few days later that a big nodule showed up in my thyroid. I thought it was cancer, but all the exams showed negative. I knew it was emotional, that my symptoms were all from my energy body, and from the immeasurable grief and guilt I felt. I hadn't been there for her. She had always been there for me.

I continued to homeschool my three children, going through the motions of life. All I could think was, "I am going to figure this out. My grandmother's life will not be in vain. She lived her life for me and my sister. I will honor her by finding the key to fulfillment."

I've been told countless times that "This is it. Life on earth is suffering. When you get to heaven, you'll be happy." This is coding. We have all been coded. Coding can be changed intentionally with awareness and energy healing. Even though I have been in countless workshops and completed several certification programs, it was experiencing energy work and sisterhood that catapulted me into incredible self-love and personal responsibility. I was ready. I had God. And He showed up *big*. After I joined a Mastermind and surrounded myself with women living in love and possibility, everything in me woke up and lined up.

Privately, I became obsessed with learning about frequency, vibration, and energy. I started seeing myself as a vortex and a portal. I asked God for a clean, clear channel to hear Him. I couldn't hear Him because of all the limiting beliefs expressed by the voices in my head. They're usually loud and loaded with self-preservation, protection, and fear. But they aren't me.

To strengthen my channel, I started to practice heart and brain coherence, heart breathing, grounding, and the infusion of water with intention. I became grateful for all the past versions of myself and realized my body had been carrying a load that needed to be put down to accelerate what I came here for.

I have been coded with many wonderful codes, but also with scarcity, difficulty, unworthiness, and pain. These frequencies stop with me. Not under my watch will my kids inherit. Some codes are expired and no longer serve a purpose. Some codes are gifts that I receive, cherish, and by choice will pass down to my children. Those codes are frequencies. There's no more room to question our worthiness. Doubt itself is an expired code. When I know I am, then can I receive.

We are very good with the coding of giving but not so much with the code of receiving. I started to practice receiving. When someone messaged me something positive about myself, I messaged back the words: "I receive it, thank you!" What happened next is that my friends started to text me the same words and we created a culture of celebration and receivership.

Believe that you can receive a clear channel so God and spirit can communicate as one, straight to and through you.

I used to hate selling. I was so insecure. I had a fear of judgment about my prices, my services, and my products. I wished I could do everything for free. So I did. I dried up very quickly, and so did my finances, because there was no energy coming back to me. I then reframed: "Selling is an energetic gift; if I don't sell, others can't receive the gift. I am not selling this. I am the embodiment of what I know works." I was only able to do that because I recoded myself. I loved myself and became self-deserving rather than self-sacrificing. All the parts of me were in alignment with each other, with all of me. I knew then that there's nothing more important and valuable than myself. And if I could be congruent in this truth, in this new alignment, I could effortlessly expand this frequency to my children, my music, and my clients.

It's true. When you are aligned in high frequency, your entire world changes and everyone in it feels it. It is the domino effect of abundance. Once I leaned into the pain, it led me to the greatest prize: falling in love with myself by honoring my design. I no longer need to accept misalignment in my body or anywhere in my life.

I keep frequencies around that remind me I am abundance and abundant. I choose to be surrounded by those who support me in higher frequency and alignment, people who speak to my greatness. Now that I am aware, I speak to my DNA with gratitude for those who came before me. I recode and activate all that God put inside of me as pure possibility, love, and purpose.

If this resonates, I invite you in love to take aligned action. If you wait, you will lose the momentum of the frequency of the *new knowing*.

Kenya Evelyn lives in Nashville, Tennessee, with her three kids and husband of seventeen years. She is passionate about God, her family, and awakening the truth of our light and the power of our being. A lifelong singer and certified music therapist, energy healer, health coach, and life coach, she calls herself an Intuitive Frequency Alchemist. She teaches others how to harmonize their energy, vibration, and frequency to achieve a life of fun, fulfillment, and purpose—what she calls *wealth*—through aligned frequency. Kenya believes in creating stronger families and supporting women who love themselves so unconditionally that everything they touch is calibrated with the frequency of abundance. She creates with ease and flow; hosts retreats and singing circles; provides one-on-one coaching; facilitates "Night of Healing" and "Frequency Codes." She invites you to reclaim your voice, find your rhythm, learn your frequencies, discover your divine design, and amplify your power through voice and movement. For a special gift to *Align* readers, visit:

www.kenyaevelyn.com/align
www.kenyacvclyn.com
www.facebook.com/kenya.evelyn.7/
www.instagram.com/frequency.alchemist/

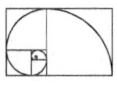

Dr. Steven Klayman, DC

Fix Your Own Ass

and Other Things Too

When I was attending The City College of New York, there was absolutely no indication that I would become a doctor and go on to witness healing miracles. My life was mainly about golf, girls, and marijuana. I played golf in high school and college, then turned pro. My first professional tournament was a disaster. It was a small local event with small prize money, and I was terribly outclassed by some really good players. It didn't take a degree in rocket science to figure out if I continued along this path, I was going to be very, very hungry.

It turns out that it was quite fortuitous for my golf tournament experience to have been unsuccessful. I just didn't know at that time that there were better things planned for me. I started my chiropractic practice in Texas many years ago. Every couple of weeks, somebody says to me, "You're not retiring soon, are you?" I guess I must be starting to look old. It doesn't feel like it's been that many years because the work still feels fresh. I feel great. My health is good, and I have no intention of retiring. In fact, I told a patient last week, "When you are doing this type of work, you never retire."

Every day in my office, miraculous things happen. The main reason people go into the medical field is to alleviate others' suffering. Somewhere along the way, money gets involved, burnout happens, rules and regulations get instituted, and it becomes a mundane job checking boxes on a computer or justifying treatment protocol to a bureaucratic insurance adjuster. It's happened to thousands of doctors. Doctors are fleeing the health field in record numbers, especially with the advent of electronic health records, which drive them crazy. I've gotten frustrated but have stayed in my practice because of all I have learned and because of my ability to both benefit my patients and teach others.

What I learned is that separating the spiritual aspect of a human being from the physical aspect is similar to trying to separate wetness from water. I don't believe it can be done. Spirituality is an inherent part of our nature. The kind, compassionate, and loving aspect of our nature may be deeply suppressed, but it is in all of us, even the most disillusioned. I feel my growth as a healer has paralleled my spiritual growth. Each aspect reinforces the other. I frequently call on the aspect of the Divine that does healing to help me or guide me with the patient. I rely on my Divine not just for healing other people but also for my own life. I talk to my Divine as I would talk to a friend in a very genuine and sincere manner.

A few years ago I was very upset with my Divine for not answering my prayer. Standing before my altar, I yelled, expressing my displeasure at His poor performance. I got on my motorcycle, a 600-pound Kawasaki ZX-14, and went to a friend's house for our meditation group. When I arrived home at ten thirty that evening, I lifted the garage door and walked the motorcycle inside. I did not realize I hadn't put the kickstand down all the way, and as I leaned the bike over, it fell and knocked me to the floor. I was not hurt, but now I had a 600-pound motorcycle lying on its side in the garage. It was too late at night to call my neighbor. For some reason, I leaned over and grabbed the handlebars as if I could lift this bike up myself. I was in the perfect position to blow out all the disks in my back. But as I tried to lift the bike, it came up effortlessly. It was as if it were a Schwinn bicycle weighing twenty pounds. It didn't even take much effort for me to lift all 600 pounds.

Let's be clear: there is no way I could lift 600 pounds by myself. I knew what had happened. My Divine, who is always with me, as he or she is always with you, was letting me know that He/She appreciated my genuineness earlier that day by lifting my motorcycle for me. While I do not see angels or experience past lives or any of the other dramatic spiritual experiences that some people have, I do get direct help when I really need it. Prayers that are important to me are frequently answered. My Divine lets me know I am not alone, and it is never more obvious than when I'm in the office trying to help someone with their health.

As I look back along my journey, I see times when I came to a fork in the road where a decision was required. Because I chose a particular direction, events ensued, and I am compelled to reflect on why and how beautifully things occurred.

It's the same for each of us. Had you not broken up with your girlfriend, you wouldn't have gone to the bar where you met your wife. Had you not been fired from a job, you would never have applied to the job that you subsequently got, where you earned a greater income. There are countless times in our lives when we somehow made the correct decision. I believe that those events are when we were pushed by our Divine for our own benefit.

An important event in my life was meeting Jami in India in 2008. I helped treat her celiac disease. Around 2018, I talked to Jami while she was in Australia doing her healing practice. She told me that after I treated her in 2008, she was so impressed that she called my mentor, Dr. Victor L. Frank DC, NMD, in the United States and told him that she wanted to learn Total Body Modification (TBM), a diagnostic tool and system for treating a wide variety of ailments. He said to her, "I've been waiting for you to call."

As it turns out, I was an impetus in her life. She told me that when she came back from spending time with Dr. Frank in the United States, her healing and diagnostic abilities had taken a quantum leap. She was now doing long-distance healing through her website and making a significant income. She asked me if I was doing any long-distance healing. I told her I had learned how to diagnose long-distance many years before, but I'd never really used it. Jami challenged me to do to long-distance healings in my office the coming week. It works*. I teach the philosophical and practical aspects of how to do this in my seminars. * *this information is intended for educational purposes only, if you have a medical condition please consult a health professional. It is not intended to diagnose, treat or cure any illness.*

You do not have to be an extraordinary healer to apply these techniques; in fact, some of them simply require knowing the anatomy and the underlying laws of nature that hold the consciousness and the anatomy together. It's just that there are other laws of nature at work that some of us have discovered, and some have yet to discover.

I teach individuals how to do things so they can create healing miracles in their homes and offices. It's knowledge that needs to be shared, and I am happy to share what I've learned and experienced. One of the more enjoyable parts of my professional activities is teaching a seminar that I call "Fix Your Own Ass," otherwise known as "Techniques in Self-Healing."

What would it be like if you could go to the grocery store and test the supplements on yourself or find a solution for a particular problem? That is part of what we teach in the seminar, along with the difference between disk-caused back pain and vertebral-caused back pain, and how to self-treat asthma, acid reflux, knee pain, plantar fasciitis, headaches, and hemorrhoids. One of the attributes of participating in the seminars is learning to be more self-reliant about your health, and finding easy solutions to health problems your doctor doesn't know about.

This all occurred because I went to India in 2005 in a lot of pain, and was healed. I went to a local medical practitioner and became very curious about the technique he used to relieve my neck pain and the pain radiating into my index fingers. I walked into the office, and he stood up to greet me, the top of his head hitting at about my sternum.

"You sit," he said. Then he mumbled while touching my shoulder. He told me to go home and come back in two days. I experienced half the pain that night that I'd been experiencing. When I went back, I asked him if he would teach me what he did, and he said, "Yes!" I was astounded, but that episode amped up my healing abilities. I was given a gift.

Virtual healing has aligned my professional growth with my spiritual purpose, and I am grateful I had the foresight to listen and learn from others who understood the power of healing techniques and consciousness development. I have a moral obligation to help people get well rapidly and inexpensively. I'd love to share this with you.

▼ ▼ ▼ ▼ ▼

Dr. Steven Klayman, DC is a chiropractor living in Austin, Texas. A 1980 graduate of Palmer College of Chiropractic, Dr. Klayman has studied with many leaders in his field, including Dr. Victor Frank, DC, ND, who developed much of the Total Body Modification (TBM) program, a kinesiology-based system of health care treating a broad range of conditions. Dr. Klayman coinvented the TBM Allergy Correction Technique, which is taught worldwide, and the Pelvic Balancer, a device patients can use to correct pelvic imbalance and sacroiliac joint pain at home. He teaches the seminar "Fix Your Own Ass, and Other Things Too." It is designed to teach patients simple methods that work at home and to foster self-reliance.

www.klaymanholisticchiro.com/

"Build your tribe
then be
your tribe."

— Mistilei

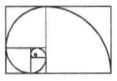

Savannah Gates

Magia

I am in it right now. I am in the "in-between" or the "middle," as my dear belated friend, Valerie Doshier, called it. During her last days spent wavering between realms, she left us with the words, "Do not sway my sweet, sweet soul; do not sway. Do not find yourself anywhere near the middle." I have spent years wondering what she meant by that, turning the phrase over and over to examine it from every angle. It was not until I wrote it into this chapter that it finally caught the light just right.

My family dropped everything to move to the small town of Granbury, Texas, to open a coffee and wine bar with friends in the fall of 2019, which finally opened fall of 2020 following the peak of the pandemic. "What a waste," they said, as we left Amarillo with the U-Haul. There were two major, undisclosed layers of reason that contributed to this seemingly rash decision for someone with an engineering background to shapeshift into a barista. The first was sensing an alignment opportunity for my exceptionally gifted other half, Chef Rose Pebbles. I was aware there would be a lack of technical intellect and overall stimulation for myself, so the second, and less apparent, justification was the abundant access to people, or rather people having access to me.

I believe that the right people will find you at the right time. The question is whether you are in a state of awareness and reception. I would be managing a space built on the principle of classic community. Therefore, by design, I would be practicing service, awareness, and reception daily for whomever walked through the front door. The leap had nothing to do with my love for coffee and wine being in alignment with what I "should" or wanted to be doing. I could not find alignment, but my ability to run a business revolving around a common love for coffee and wine enabled me to step back and give the Universe space to manifest, while cultivating the sparkling career of my up-and-coming Chef.

I had been hunting alignment for many years, seeking the balance of what breathed life into me, paid the bills, and fulfilled the yearning to make an immense impact in the world. After repeated soul-aching cycles, I was ready to sit still and listen. As my favorite theoretical physicist and respected friend, Stefan Estreicher, calls them, "interesting people" began to trickle through the door. With years of practice and soaking up lessons from mentors, I have developed the ability to distinguish the "interesting people." Many have grown from guests to friends, and some even to family. They have filled my cup with laughter, hope, and love, and I will forever owe them gratitude.

Fall of 2021, I asked a friend if I could contribute an article to her newly acquired magazine. She and the editor planned to add an educational piece to enrich the journal, while I desired to broaden my audience for education on farm-to-table. I had not written anything more in depth than a menu since technical writing during my engineering career years before. In fact, I loathed English class so much that I completed all my college credits during high school so I could close that door indefinitely. For this piece, I did not have a plan. I blindly sensed opportunity and seized it. A rough draft flowed out of me like water and was complete within hours. The editor unexpectedly blew up the polished product onto six stunning pages, as it quickly became the favorite piece within that edition. I was repeatedly asked how many months I had spent researching to develop the content, and I responded with a puzzled face, "I did not research anything. I wrote this in a couple days." Feedback received could be summarized as "awe."

Recognizing that the power and potential were growing organically and rapidly, I detected a tingle of something I had not felt in years. I did not have a word for it. In fact, I did not even speak of it, for fear I would scare it away. I was asked to become a permanent fixture in the magazine, and with every article, impact both on myself and the readers intensified. By the third publication, I had opened my mind and soul to the possibility that the Universe may be inviting me to be a writer, and then…"the magic people" began to come through the door. By "the magic people" I mean the people in tune with and operating by the magic we are each born with but often forget along the way. Their frequency was different, and I felt the resonance instantly. Conversations were held both verbally and between the lines.

First was Melissa Collins, the singer-songwriter whom I had hired for live music on a hunch. She had just begun her journey back to music and was looking for someone to cowrite. She liked my writing style in the magazines, knew I had interest in music, and thought there might be something there. I did not have much confidence in myself, considering she was in the Grammy Book and that I had blocked out the music within me long before. I was wrong. The first time I tried to sit down and write a song, more than enough lyrics for a full track came out on paper within a few hours. It took her less than that to respond with music for the words. I did not know what expectations a seasoned professional held for the songwriting process, so I had no choice but to operate by flow. The magic developed far faster than I could have imagined. Endorphins and a levitating sensation, tingling in my hands and a flood of creativity. Poetry, music, ideas, and dreams all came pouring through. It was a familiar high, like flying a hot air balloon—floating with the current but simultaneously so electrifying and radiant that anyone in the room became addicted to the air around me. We even named it: *Magia*.

Next to burst through the door was *the* Dr. Julie Howard, whom I rapidly developed a deep, multifaceted connection with. She was followed by a travel writer, an international bestselling author, a film script writer, a prominent figure in the music industry, and artists of all kinds, all wandering through the door within weeks of each other, some within hours. I was invited to collaborate and was offered services by all of them. Half had no idea of my background or that I wrote at all. They simply felt they were in the right place at the right time and proposed intuitively.

The surge grew, powerful enough that it ignited an undeniable demand for growth within everyone in reach, like a wildfire blazing out of control. Even if it was just for a month, it was real, and it was pure magic. But not everyone understands magic. It can be scary to those who have never felt alignment from the inside and do not embrace losing control. It can shatter friendships and challenge relationships of all kinds. This was my experience, and I had to make choice a priority: a choice to continue dancing in the flames or to preserve my family unit and find a safer way to align. After a month of raw rapture, I made the choice to choke it down again and return to misalignment until I could find another way.

As I said, I am in it right now…my least favorite place to be, the "middle." Here, there is so much back and forth, up and down, all around. Many days it feels like I am trying to decode a secret to unlock my own life. Other days I recognize that the "in-between" is also a place of hope, as I remind myself of the power of gratitude. I no longer have my switch flipped in the off position, and for that I am grateful. As dim and frustrating as it may seem, the light is flickering now, and that is more light than the darkness I sat in for so long. Sometimes the shifts from defeat to hope and back again toggle within minutes, without warning. Other cycles last for days. There is no formula for it, no controlling it. All I can do is step back to gain a greater picture of what is happening, dig for the roots of both negative and positive, breathe, and do "the next right thing," as Anna serenades in *Frozen II*.

Alignment is personal. The ego likes to suggest otherwise, but *you* are the only instrument that *you* can tune. I have learned that "the next right thing" is *not* trying to will alignment for someone else, no matter how close that person is to me and how clear my vision for them appears to be. Sometimes becoming aware of what is wrong is as equally compelling as the aha moment for what is right.

The noise is the worst. It is so loud inside my head. It feels like endless war with no rhyme or reason. I imagine it being a microdose of the Vietnam jungle during the seventies, with maps of emotional mine-fields belonging to friends, family, and even acquaintances: calculations of which choice is the least bad; replayed screaming from unexpected explosions of hostility and abandonment by loved ones; ringing in my ears from deafening silence where there should be poetry, music, ideas, and dreams. All this, but at least *now I am fighting for me.* And for the light. At least now I remember that the light exists, and it exists inside me. At least now I have felt a moment of alignment, like a bear basking in the sun after a long winter, or a genie stretching after centuries in a lamp. Now, I have a goal. To find that again, because "that" leads to finding me. Like a tracking dog, I caught a fresh whiff of my target after ages with only a dull memory, at best. The weaving feels like a drunk swaying in the streetlamp glow, slowly stumbling a less than straight line home. The headaches are hard. And they change from day to day, so I cannot discern between dehydration, stress, or my pituitary begging to open. I get snapshots of clarity that light the path, just enough to know I am still on it.

It feels isolated and takes effort to be mindful that the Universe is all intertwined, so I am truly never alone. When I listen, there are radio signals screaming guidance at me. Some of it is lucid. Some of it I recognize as indicators, but they seem to be in other languages. I have spent time reflecting on chapters in my life when there was less noise. Late nights in the dorm fourteen years ago, writing random thoughts in a small, black paperback notebook while everyone else slept. Those random thoughts seemed impossible theories of the Universe. Last week, I learned that those random thoughts were aligned with innovative technology being born, developed, and actively practiced for immense healing by Dr. Jeffrey Thompson. What do I do with that new profound knowledge? What was I doing differently at eighteen that allowed such high-frequency theories to flow through me? How do I return to that? It feels like calibrating a receiver.

My diet is far better, I have recommitted to exercise, and I get fresh air and time in the sun (but not enough). I am resting sufficiently. Time away from the noise and alone time at two a.m. in the music hall are missing. Awe and wonder are lacking. Laughter is infrequent. Spontaneity is rare. Too much time on my phone seeking infinity outwardly and not enough time pursuing infinity inwardly. Breathing. Just breathing.

Here I am, swaying in the middle. I know the only way out is through, so I wrote this chapter for you.

Savannah Gates was born in Las Cruces, New Mexico, and raised in the tiny agricultural community of Bushland, Texas, with her younger sister, Chloe Gates, DVM. They roamed free on West Texas acreage with only the limits of their imaginations. Their parents, Steve and Janice Gates, and older sister, Kim Gates, were self-made professionals and insisted the girls could grow up to be anything they set their mind to. Savannah took that quite literally and has recreated herself many times since graduating from Texas Tech in 2012 with a bachelor's degree in mechanical engineering. From military helicopters and weapons to coffee and cocktails, energy sector program management to farming, fine-dining experience innovation to international consulting, and as writer and mother, Savannah's lens through life continues to develop. She sees a deep-rooted connection among her experiences and pursues the vortex. Her perseverance is accredited to the love and support of her family and close friends.

www.Savannah-Gates.com
www.allthingsamos.org/

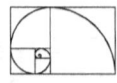

Ryan Williams

Watering Family Trees

A Generational Journey

As the child of a semi-absent parent who evolved into a fully absent parent, I spent many years of my youth questioning the decisions of my elders. Here's what I mean when I say semi-absent: when you are in active addiction, you cannot be fully present within your family. You show your child something else is more important than they are every day. Your denial does not whisper to your children's reality like it does to your own; your addiction does not validate your mistakes to them the way it does and/or did to yourself. This may not be easy to accept, but it is true.

At this time, my father is completely absent. His addiction to drugs and his infatuation with his own pride have come between any relationship he's ever been able to have with anyone. I had to eventually release him from his fabricated role as my protector and free him of any expectation of being my willing patriarch in this life. Each excuse for why he could not be that man for me just added to the weight of my personal longing for and loathing of him.

Currently, my mother is fully present. While she also battled learning to fill that all-encompassing void within in the form of addiction or the pursuit of love from men who did not know how to, she has made exceptional headway in finding herself and not making excuses as to why she couldn't always fully show up for us. I'm proud of where we are today as mother and daughter. There was a time in my adolescence when I was uncertain if our bond would be strengthened and ameliorate over time, or wither away into a mirrored reflection of the substandard relationship she shares with her own mother today.

Experiencing high levels of disappointment and feeling unworthy at a young age amplified my ability to pick out any little sign that I was unloved or unlovable—regardless of whether those signs were real or somewhere just outside of truth. I'm trying to heal my inner child, the one who was formed by absent or semi-absent parents. The lack of relationship has bred such unnecessary emotional challenges in my adult life. The ability to trust without question, to fully believe in my own self-worth without feeling like a fraud, to feel worthy of true love or to believe it could ever be given to me, to trust anyone with my full vulnerability, to break the cycle of addiction and self-inflicted pain within myself—these are the challenges. I have spent more than a decade doing the emotional, physical, and mental work to heal myself, for myself. I know there is still a journey ahead.

While I have made progress and defied many statistics (a feat I remind myself to be proud of daily), there are continual challenges. One of the hardest is that there is no designated finish line. This is a forever thing. Some days are way smoother than others.

I acknowledge the subpar experiences of my childhood are no excuse for poor behavior and that history is no excuse for an unfulfilled present or ill-fated future, but having constant and proper parental love certainly never hurt anyone quite as much as not having it did. That deserves acknowledgment. Questions swirl in my psyche any time I think of the man who gave me half his DNA to bring me into existence. How can a parent not know? How can they simply dismiss that their reckless choices, their hierarchy of ego, their solution of abandonment, has caused detrimental harm to their child(ren)? How can that be ignored? Doesn't it gnaw at them every waking moment? I believe that inside every burning adult there lives a sobbing child pleading for the love of their creators.

Would you not embrace a wet-cheeked child with arms outstretched if it meant you had to be challenged to fully open your own?

Today, my soul resides in a twenty-nine-year-old body, a body previously presumed to be incapable of gravidity, a body that is now carrying and growing a little boy we get to meet in just three short months. Becoming his mother has changed something inside me. Not just on the physical plane, but spiritually. As a parent-to-be, I can't imagine anything or anyone ever taking me away from my child. Not voluntarily. Certainly not because I prefer an addiction. He is my blood, my legacy, my truest little love, the soul I carry in my body, the body I nourish at the sacrifice of my own, the person who will look to me for guidance and love until long past my final breath.

More than ever before, I'm asking how someone can create a life, manifest consciousness, hold such a sacred bond, and yet choose to not fully participate in that destiny. A child deserves a mother and father, balanced, dancing in equal amounts of responsibility, after bringing their creation onto the earth. For me, this brings an entirely new definition of what it means for a man and a woman to "make love" with one another. What could possibly be more important than this? What could ever be more important than knowing when your soul leaves this world that you have imprinted a legacy of forgiveness, acceptance, love, and hope in the lives of the family tree you continued to grow? To know with no doubts that your branch in that tree is strong enough and secured with enough love to hold every beautiful flower that buds from it. That it continues to nurture every seedling even after your time has passed.

The life lessons children are taught today, whether intentionally or through fallacy, are the lessons they will teach their children tomorrow. This is the ripple effect. It can bring generational healing or perpetuate trauma. This is where forgiveness comes into play. No one is immune to the undulation of past generations. Statistically speaking, children are more likely to be like every ancestor before them than they are to manifest a new disposition, whether they are propagated from love or from pain. However, there is still a choice: a choice to break free from the weighty fetters that restricted every primogenitor before from achieving delectation and sovereignty.

I learned that I have the power, solidarity, and fortitude to start a new wavelet in this pool of genealogical angst. By unearthing awareness and experiencing this enlightenment, I finally and fully feel more aligned with who I am and who I am supposed to be. This is my destiny within this family, to do my part to give our son the chance that his parents were not fully given from birth. To heal the tree that has been ailing for so many generations.

With this newfound knowledge of my true appointment, I forgive, I release, I grow, I overcome, but I still do not understand that absence of heart. That is what will break the cycle of offspring abandonment within my own bloodline. That lack of understanding is destiny manifesting into the strength to do what my ancestors could not do. To be a nurturer, lover, fighter, sister, daughter, mother, portal of consciousness, creator of true love. To take all the previous pain and displaced intentions that have exuded from one parent to the next and create the dawn of a new era for this newest descendent and for all of those who will come after him and long after me. We are meant to be the gardener and tender of the mangled tree with the guidance and lessons of all those who have watered it before. Every day is a choice; every action has a reaction. Everything I do or say from this moment on will either heal this family or continue to chip away at our exposed roots. There must be healing done from within by both parents to give a child a true opportunity to flourish and achieve their highest potential in this life.

Learning to forgive your creators for what they lacked allows you to forgive yourself for why you ache. That pain they put into you, it does not belong to you. Nor does it fully belong to them. That pain holds pieces of dark history that were never cleansed, never released, never cured, and thus replanted within the spirit of every child swimming in the aftermath of that affliction. Release it. Forgive it. It does not belong to you. Find the alignment within yourself to demolish that pain and all the other emotional regrets it's brought into your life. Free yourself from the shackles of frustration and malice toward those who could not let go of that pain before you. Judge not what they could not do, only what you can do and what you choose to do with that power. It's an easier story to tell when you simply add more words to someone else's chapter and continue the same awful tale. Be the writer, the artist. Be the divine creator of your own story and write it with intent, purpose, and love.

▼ ▼ ▼ ▼ ▼

#1 International Best Selling author Ryan Williams is a person who likes to make things. Such things as: short stories, long stories, laughter, delicious meals, friendships, connections with the universe, paintings, iced coffees, funny videos, photo albums, impactful experiences, and lasting memories. She became a #1 International Best Selling author in the summer of 2022, contributing to her first anthology, *Here Comes the Sun*. This endeavor got her back in tune with what she loves to do most, create. It also inspired her to shift her career from her previous ten years in customer service and restaurant management to helping others learn how to create and have the confidence to show the world how healing creation can be and how liberating expression through literature and storytelling is. She currently resides in a small neighborhood in Oklahoma City with her German shepherd, Molly, and her three cats: Grunt, Penelope, and Artemis.

www.facebook.com/thegirlryan13

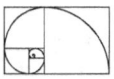

Dr. Loren Michaels Harris

I Know This Much Is True

I remember as a child hearing someone say, "We ride into this life in one vehicle, and we will ride out in that same vehicle." For what has now been sixty incredible years in this "vehicle," I can finally say regarding the previous statement, "I know this much is true!"

My vehicle, this body that contains everything I have ever needed to drive from one point within my journey to the next, has traveled a literal plethora of terrain, driven through every type of weather condition possible, and is still (I am happy to report) on the road and moving at a safe and constant speed toward its destination.

On July 4, 1962, when my vehicle was driven off of the showroom floor, it appeared to have all the customary bells and whistles: ten perfectly formed fingers, ten perfectly formed toes, big brown eyes that seemed to scan every horizon with hope and inspiration, and an incredibly animated mouth...a mouth that could transform in an instant from a soft and endearing coo to a screaming peal that could make the most seasoned of mechanics swear that there was far too much horsepower under the hood for such a small engine.

My vehicle went home that week with its original owner. The registration was in order and the title signed, as this was a cash transaction and the cost of the vehicle had already been paid in full—or so we thought. As fate would have it, I was destined to spend only a few short weeks with my original owner, Lucille. You see, although Lucille had four additional vehicles and had cared for them for many years, she found that possessing a fifth vehicle, her first 1960s model, was proving to be a bit too much to handle, so back to the dealership we went!

My second owner (her name was Ada), was a super-great mechanic who possessed five additional vehicles herself, and for some reason wanted to try her hand at completing her fleet with me. As I mentioned before, this was a cash deal for Lucille, so for her to transfer this vehicle over to Ada required nothing more than a handshake, or perhaps a hug; or maybe there was a knowing glance between these two African American single female collectors that spoke silently to the severity of this transfer of title. I don't know if in this life I will ever truly understand exactly how things went down that day—or perhaps it was night; even that I will never know—but what I do know is that for the next eleven years I was parked safely on the property of Ada, who did her best to provide me the best she had to offer. In the blink of an eye, the course of my destination was critically altered when Ada's vehicle decided to conk out. I guess her engine could not be repaired, because after that day I only saw her one other time and that was to say goodbye.

In total, this vehicle of mine was cared for, maintained by, and even in some cases used as the getaway car by twenty-two different women. I know this much is true: that was then, and this is now.

Today, as I look back through the maintenance records, the traffic citations, the insurance claims, etc. (in other words, "the paperwork") associated with my journey thus far, it is easier to understand why it took nearly fifty years to go out and procure my own Kelley Blue Book.

See, here's the deal: in my twenties, I drove everywhere out of fear and desperation. I drove like a bat out of hell (literally). I allowed my tires to bald (and eventually my hair followed suit, but that's another story). I allowed all my vital fluid levels to drop, and my wiper blades were for shit. You get the picture? I simply did not value vehicle upkeep. I was young, and the world owed me, so fuck it…I'd ride this bitch until the wheels fell off. And fall off they did.

In my thirties (which I never thought I would live to see), I continued my careless off-roading. I picked up tons of hitchhikers, loaned my vehicle out to strangers, and never gave any of it a second thought because, after all, it's not like I was going to live into my forties. It was in my thirties that I skip-traced my way back to Lucille, my original owner. I distinctly remember thinking, "This is it. Now that I have been reunited with my original owner, I'll finally be back to my shiny showroom floor self!"

I could not have been more wrong.

Sometimes when we think we are beginning to care, that is when we realize the fear—the fear we possess regarding finally looking beneath the hood of our vehicles. It is this fuel of fear that causes every single function within our vehicles to fail. It took well into my forties to realize the damage I had endured due to a series of fender benders, rear-endings, and you name it. I finally looked at my dashboard and realized that the fuel light was on and that there were maintenance alerts all over the place. Alerts that I had somehow never noticed before.

I hit my fifties with my pedal to the metal! I am determined to raise the blue book value of my journey. I am dedicated to using my high beams to finally illuminate the terrain, and for the first time in all the time I have been on the road, I find myself admiring the sleek design of my vehicle. One day I catch a glimpse of my fresh paint job in a window and suddenly, just like that, it all makes sense; I have officially become a classic! How could I have ever known that one day the world would be thirsty to learn from the story of this vehicle how to create their own Divine Design, how to become—yes, you guessed it—a classic?

Yet today, that is exactly the reality of my vehicle. I drive for a living now. I guess you could say that although I am a classic, I am not one of those vehicles that remains in storage most of the year, only getting out into the world at large once, maybe twice per year. We all know those types of classics, who love when admirers come to them but are not so keen on road trips themselves. I use my vehicle today in much the way one sees an Uber or Lyft: a great way to get somewhere.

But I really need to get back to the point in this story where we were discussing maintenance records. Remember how I mentioned I seemed to have all of the paperwork that would allow me to piece together memories from all of the neighborhoods I have driven through, parked in, or escaped from? Those records allowed me to find my way back to my original owner. The story was placed back within context after so many years of "versions" running the show. The healing was unleashed the moment I found the maintenance records.

On July 4, 2022, this vehicle turned sixty years old. If I had a chance to go back in time and change anything about my journey or the way in which I cared for my vehicle, would I? How many of us have spent countless hours, days, weeks, years even, asking ourselves that very question?

Ten years ago, I would have had a mile-long list of reasons for the many mistakes I thought I had made in life. Ten years ago, I would have told you that no matter what you try to do in order to get to that place in life where you are valued, it won't happen. Ten years ago, this vehicle was out of alignment.

Remember back in the day, the take-your-hands-off-the-wheel test? We would do that to test how the vehicle would react. Would it swerve to one side or the other? Would the vehicle stay true and remain within its lane? If you have ever attempted this test of removing your hands from the steering wheel, then you already know it can be the most thrilling thing when the vehicle remains true to its lane and does not falter in either direction. And you most surely know that it can just as easily be terrifying if the vehicle should suddenly swerve to the left into oncoming traffic, or to the right just where there is no guardrail and a thousand-foot drop is inevitable.

Having courage to take our hands off the wheel is found buried deep within the desire to live our best life. Having courage to pour over the maintenance records of our journeys is nestled within the confines of a thirsty soul. Having courage to acknowledge and then celebrate the entire trip log is waiting within the healing of forgiveness. Having courage to "become" is guaranteed within your birthright known as legacy. Anything that does not serve you must go!

Keep your vehicle in alignment with purpose. Whatever you say, mean it, and it shall become meaningful somewhere in the Universe.

Never forget: you rode into this life as a classic and you can ride out as an even greater version of the original, but only if you write your own blue book, show the world your worth, and leave the world your value. Live with your tank full. Die with your tank empty. This is Purpose! I know this much is true.

Dr. Loren Michaels Harris strives to motivate, inspire, and uplift every person who crosses his path. As a former foster child, he overcame extreme challenges throughout his life and discovered a practical approach for building purpose. Loren is the host of *Bathrobe Moments*, a daily interview talk show focusing on Illuminated Conversations, which has been a passion for Dr. Harris for six years, airing five days per week for fifty straight weeks every year and featured on the e360tv Network, where Loren also serves as an executive producer. As a mentor, Purpose Discovery Coach, author, and TV presenter, Loren has been heard on *Larry King Live* and *NPR*, featured in *PEOPLE Magazine*, and seen on ABC, NBC, CBS, CNN, and Fox. Currently, Loren is featured on the covers of *SHIFT Magazine* (as the first openly gay service member and the first African American man to grace this magazine's cover), *Heart Of Hollywood Magazine*, *Global Achievers Magazine*, and *Courageous Men Magazine*.

Loren believes in giving back and in never offering the world what he refers to as "zero calorie content." He is the founder of The Power of WE Symposium, which celebrates underserved kids of color in desperate areas around the country. Keeping with his entrepreneurial passions, Loren works with an elite group of coaching clients in honing their Divine Purpose and then taking that Purpose into the world. Slam The Hammer Mastermind, LMH Coaching Rockstars, and Loren's Elevate masterclass are all paths where he utilizes his gifts through a "paying it forward" mindset. Loren's motto is "You do the work, and I will provide the stages!" He is one-half of "The Diversity Duo" on the partnership podcast *Licensed For Love: The Heartbeat In Relationship Conversation* with his cohost Jax

Young, a Nashville country music artist. Loren recently wrapped up the filming of his first movie experience *Heathen,* a made-for-television movie which will air on Peacock in winter of 2022.

Loren's Goalcast video can be viewed on YouTube:
www.youtube.com/watch?v=NHeQafrmpG8
You can connect with Loren through his website,
www.Lorenmichaelsharris.com, or on any of his other social media platforms.

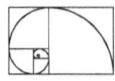

Mistilei Wriston

The *Hole* Truth
and nothing but the truth

Alignment boils down to being honest: fully, wholly honest. For the sake of this story, it's about minding my "holes" with honesty. Stay with me! I know people don't like the word *hole*, and here I am talking about my *hole truth*, starting with my *mouth hole,* which is always getting me into trouble, sometimes for what it ate and sometimes for what it says.

For thirty years, I studied, experimented with, and taught the most grueling diets. I was an eager student, but my weight always came back eventually. Always! I had similar ups and downs with business. I would achieve just enough to seem successful and yet I was always on the edge of a struggle. Even in relationships, I would find the most incredible, magical human and fall madly and passionately in love, only to realize a few months later there was not enough truth present for me to even know IF we were in love. There were many areas like this; however, my weight was an ongoing focus. I had more success than most "dieters". It was a constant struggle.

I was at a point in life when things were not, as they say, going as planned. Exhausted, feeling like I had bottomed out, I went into a meditation with a different mindset. I surrendered. I had tried it all, but I could not master this body and get it to a point where I could love it. I surrendered. I needed some clarity because there was no way this was what a successful life felt like. I have a friend who once told me his life feels like plain water. I love water, and yet I knew that feeling. I felt it when I first got sober. Super-duper proud to be sober, but bored and lifeless. It sucked. Dieting sucked. It all sucked. So, I surrendered. I went into meditation with the intention of solving the mystery of my weight and my sucky life. From this surrender, a promise was made in meditation between *Self* and *Self*. The message was crystal clear. It seemed too simple, too good to be true. I wrote the message down, and although I was skeptical of my own meditation, I was committed to surrendering. I stayed in the space and looked at the words that had come to me:

You can eat anything you want, anytime you want, as much as you want, if you eat real food when your body can receive it and you are honest of the why.

I have spent many hours in meditation with this sentence since then. I've dissected each word and letter. I began to ask myself about what "food" I ate. I moved to what my children call Eating Ingredients. I made my food. Because I didn't know what was in the wrapper they handed me in the drive-through, I could not honestly say if it was real food; in fact, I knew damn well it wasn't. So rather than hit the drive-through when I forgot my lunch, I had to go *into* the grocery store and buy a container of blueberries and a bag of pistachios or other ingredients to nourish myself until I could make my meal and be better prepared.

Accountability is a key to alignment. I was known to have an avocado, a spoon, and a vial of salt in my bag during this time. I cooked what I wanted, using the best ingredients possible. Meal preparation became an activity with music and phone calls with friends. I was eating more delicious, real food, and it felt great. It felt naughty because the food was delicious. It felt like magic! Food was fun, eating was fun! My mouth hole was happy!

I began to study when a body best *receives* food and found that for myself this meant I could not eat when I was mad, sad, scared, angry, distracted, multitasking, frustrated, bored, hurried, lonely, driving, etc. I realized I ate almost exclusively in those low-energy states. I was trying to digest food, which takes a lot of energy, while in a low-energy state. I had to make changes to my life so that I could get in the right frame of mind *to eat per The Agreement*. I began to invite friends to lunch or for a casual dinner and would even call a friend to video chat while I cooked my special meal. I ordered a healthy, organic meal-prep delivery to add variety and to reduce the stress of cooking outside my comfort zone a few nights a week. I learned to be selective about my companions, as I noticed some people were not pleasant to eat around and could bring my energy down. I learned to eat in the space and energy of love.

Finally, my mouth hole was being loved and honored and treated with respect and honesty. As promised, the weight was starting to come off and I loved how I felt. I loved enjoying food again without counting and weighing and rigid rules of deprivation.

Now that my mouth hole was happy, I realized I had to pay attention to my eyes and ear holes as well. The TV in the background, the clutter lying around, the overgrown grass when I looked out the dining room window, they invoked a feeling that let me know my body was not prepared for food based on The Agreement. I removed and donated the clutter. I took the TV out. I cleaned the yard and porch and began to eat outside here and there. The beautiful sounds and visual delights in nature raised my energy. I could feel the food I ate nourishing my body as I listened to the birds chirping. I served my food on my good dinnerware and drank smoothies from fancy wine glasses. I put fresh flowers on the table. Now I was able to eat what I wanted with my mouth and I was mindful of what my eyes and ears were taking in as well. My clothes began to sag; the magic was working.

My nose was an easy next step. The more time I spent sniffing the tomatoes on the vine, the veggies in the produce aisle, and the flowers everywhere, the less I could stand the smells of artificial soaps, sprays, and products. I had used those products for years, and now I avoided the aisles that had those smells. They were no longer part of my space, and my body smelled better naturally. I took great pleasure in creating the perfect blend of essential oils for my diffuser, enjoying it throughout the day, and I switched to natural cleaning products. Now that my eyes, ears, mouth, and nose holes were being loved and treated with respect and honesty, not only were my holes elated but I was also saving money and helping the Planet!

There were obvious signs my digestion was moving along much nicer. My pee was clear, and I could get up and poop with no fuss or fanfare. At fifty-five, having had four children, I will tell you I occasionally peed when I sneezed. That stopped! I could enjoy pain-free walking with my neighbor or taking my dogs for longer walks as my energy increased. This exercise improved my gut even further. My elimination holes were happy about The Agreement, plus my pores appreciated the care I was giving to my skin holes.

With each new discovery of ways to interpret my original sentence, new worlds opened up, validating the "We don't know what we don't know" idea. I had set goals with numbers measured on a scale, or sizes on a tag, goals for what success would feel like, for what I thought it would be like if I achieved these artificial goals. I had no idea! It was like I had been looking at the menu of life, now realizing it had thousands of pages. I had only been reading the cover.

The Agreement with my body evolved and simplified over time as I saw more places it applied.

You can have *anything you want, anytime you want, as much as you want, if you are ready to receive it and are honest of the why.*

The day this iteration appeared, chills covered my entire body. It was not a weight loss secret. It was a gauge I could use *ANYWHERE!* I had already seen miraculous changes in my life. These were the uprights for my Alignment Field Goal. This is how I knew I was staying aligned with my end of the deal. I wrote it down again with important changes:

I can have anything I want, anytime I want, as much as I want, if I am ready to receive and am honest of the why.

I wanted to be skeptical, and yet it had worked every time so far. Applying it to my career and finances, I found I was unable to remember the reason I was in my industry—other than the mortgage payment needed to be paid. I knew my clients deserved someone who would be present with them. I decided to sell my home, office, and company. Was I ready to retire and have no income? No! I got honest about the money I spent and saved, and how I viewed money. My budget went from complicated and stressful to easy and elegant, despite fewer zeros in the checkbook. I removed *have to* and returned to *called to*.

I say I retired at fifty-four. That is the year I became an author, publisher, and what I have coined an Alignment Clarity Mirror for those I speak with. Some call that work. I say that I do what I love and call it alignment because *I can have anything I want, as much as I want, when I am aligned.* I knew to have what I wanted, I have to be honest and ready to receive it. I stay ready.

Currently, I'm applying The Agreement to intimate relationships. *I can have anything I want, anytime I want, as much as I want, if I am ready to receive and am honest of the why.* Honesty is a requirement, so I asked myself if I lived in such a way that I was continuously ready to meet a partner? I asked if I am the person that kind of partner would seek? For me, the message was clear: treat myself *now* the way I want the person to treat me. Present the way I want my person to present. Feed myself the way I would feed a person I was in love with (because I am!). Hold myself accountable to my spiritual practices as I would want from a partner. Maintain a space to receive a new person into my life, into my home, into my body. *Oh no! Another hole I needed to add to The Agreement.*

This one took a minute. My Self tried to argue with my Self again, and yet we knew it worked every time so far. I called my lover. I love him and have for some time. We knew we were not able to meet one another's needs or our own. We'd known that for some time as well. I explained I could no longer continue this casual thing and be honest with myself, *I am ready* to receive my person, my partner. This does not cause me misery or grief because I can now see what I have done. I hold myself accountable to stay in alignment with a beautiful gift I was given. This was the answer to all my decision-making quandaries. I can grieve my emotions for the end of our chapter *and* stay in alignment where joy resides. I understand now.

I can have any love *I want, anytime I want, as much as I want, if I am ready to receive and am honest of the why.*

The last hole, the most sacred one on my body, has the same rules as the ones up top. Living in alignment with The Agreement requires that loving my body and sharing it with another requires the same rules. It isn't about celibacy (however, it may be). I was surprised at how interesting that *honest of the why* portion of the sentence instantly silenced my arguments, back talk, and concerns. The beauty of saving this most intimate part for last is that I have seen the incredible, miraculous events that occur when I stay in alignment with The Agreement. I have absolute gratitude for the blessings the next area of accountability and growth brought to me:

I have everything I want, anytime I want, as much as I want, because I remain ready to receive and am honest of the why. I live within the lanes of alignment and pay very close attention to the edges. It is the most magical way I know to live.

With love…mind your holes at all times and live the hole truth, nothing but the truth.

Mistilei

Career entrepreneur Mistilei Wriston sold her highly ranked insurance and financial services franchise after three decades to live in nature, care for her disabled son, grow organic food, raise animals, and simplify her life. Her professional awakening created *campgroundtbd publishing*, aligning her passion and purpose. An #1 Amazon International Best-Selling author, Mistilei believes everyone has a unique story and a calling to share and connect. She recognized that honest, transparent stories change lives. Mistilei coaches those who struggle with misalignment, writer's block, addictions, and body image and behavior paralysis by removing perceived limiting beliefs and allowing a space to explore alignment. She encourages those who are ready to share their voice and write their chapter, then see it published along with other courageous and visionary individuals. The chapter is the gift to the world. The growth of each author is a gift to Mistilei. She assists with alignment virtually and with in-person retreats at her beautiful property in Western Arkansas.

calendly.com/campgroundtbd/30min
www.facebook.com/MistileiWriston/

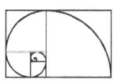

Afterword

I am humbled that your eyes have happened upon this final page.
Please feel and receive my gratitude.

Have you missed a life of alignment while looking for *it*? I almost missed out on the most incredible life because I thought *those people* were lucky. My life was different, harder. I was less likely to achieve bliss, or so I believed. I was searching for the exact place where life was perfect and I could finally be aligned like all of the lucky people. Then I realized that wasn't alignment at all. Alignment is not a point, a dot or even a line. Alignment is a space, a feeling and a path. It is a trust and love for self. It provides a sense of beautiful responsibility and pride. It looks different to everyone and is fluid even then.

I have had the privilege of working with the most giving, incredibly aligned humans on the planet: the "lucky" ones who seemed to have magic in their lives. I paid attention. I realized that even in alignment, things get messy, just significantly less! Now, *In Alignment* is the only way for me! My wish, and that of each of the authors in this book, is that you find your magic, find your lucky, find your alignment.

I offer four simple steps that have helped me even when I did not think I wanted to be helped or that anything would help. If these steps can also take you into nature, even better! I find a walk in the woods or a seat by my pond erases a lot of my writer's block or, at the very least, makes it less important for a time.

The Steps

Step One: Spill the words in your head onto actual paper. Whatever you are thinking about, write it down. It can be your grocery list, your to-do list, a favorite poem or scripture, lyrics to a song, what your neighbor did that irked you–just dump it all out! Like me, you may find all the words dancing in your imagination and thoughts that are held captive can be maddening. Step one, spill! If you draw a blank, write about anyone or anything that makes you feel grateful! Keep the words flowing. This will also help your brain "think" differently. Allow your brain to access vocabulary you haven't used in a while. Stir up those sleepy creative neurons. Find synonyms for the words you really want, wish, desire or crave to express. Finally, even if all you've written down is the grocery list, jazz it up with your delicious, mouth-watering words.

Step Two: Release your frustration. When you are ready, write one thing that is bothering or confusing you; a struggle, a goal, a dream, a wish. Start with generalities and then get specific. If possible, stay present with a single topic; explore the facts and emotions surrounding it and pay attention to how they are interacting. If you get sidetracked, come back to your topic. Then, when you are ready, stop writing and rest.

Step Three: Rewrite the story with YOUR ending. Make it exactly as you desire it to be! Get specific about what it looks like, smells like, feels like in this new version. Write as many endings as you can think of! Add comedy and use words that make the story hilarious. Write science fiction, romance, postcards.

Step Four: Repeat as needed. The goal is not to end up with perfectly written, or even legible pages. The goal is to purge a bit of the extra noise you carry around in your mind, to invite clarity and peace to enter into your real-life story and ignite that little light in your head so it can shine unfiltered, unfettered. You and your brain can solve a lot of issues once that noise settles down.

This is how writing helps me. I hope you will allow it to help you as well. I have an incredible editor and writing coach, Cheryl Roberts Oliver. I am not a writing coach. I am a woman who coaches people to *Live, Love Nature, and to Write*. I help publish those that are ready for the challenge, either electronically or in person at our new location in Western Arkansas. Write where you are or come write with us! I am at a beautiful place where my passion, purpose, and profession intersect. I hope that by reading the amazing stories and hearing the voices featured in this book, you will find your own words falling magically onto paper.

With love,
Mistilei

campgroundtbd@gmail.com
campgroundtbd.com
www.facebook.com/MistileiWriston